Omar's Interpreter; A New Life of Edward FitzGerald

Adams, Morley, Ainger, Alfred

Copyright © BiblioLife, LLC

BiblioLife Reproduction Series: Our goal at BiblioLife is to help readers, educators and researchers by bringing back in print hard-to-find original publications at a reasonable price and, at the same time, preserve the legacy of literary history. The following book represents an authentic reproduction of the text as printed by the original publisher and may contain prior copyright references. While we have attempted to accurately maintain the integrity of the original work(s), from time to time there are problems with the original book scan that may result in minor errors in the reproduction, including imperfections such as missing and blurred pages, poor pictures, markings and other reproduction issues beyond our control. Because this work is culturally important, we have made it available as a part of our commitment to protecting, preserving and promoting the world's literature.

All of our books are in the "public domain" and some are derived from Open Source projects dedicated to digitizing historic literature. We believe that when we undertake the difficult task of re-creating them as attractive, readable and affordable books, we further the mutual goal of sharing these works with a larger audience. A portion of BiblioLife profits go back to Open Source projects in the form of a donation to the groups that do this important work around the world. If you would like to make a donation to these worthy Open Source projects, or would just like to get more information about these important initiatives, please visit www.bibliolife.com/opensource.

Omar's Interpreter
A new Life of Edward FitzGerald

by

Morley Adams

With an Essay on the Letters
by
Canon Ainger

Third and cheaper edition

LONDON
THE PRIORY PRESS HAMPSTEAD
1911

All rights reserved.

PREFACE TO NEW EDITION.

OMAR'S INTERPRETER, having passed through two editions, it is evident that a demand exists for what I may perhaps designate a FitzGerald primer. The publishers, therefore, have decided to re-issue my book in a cheaper form.

The former somewhat exclusive circle of Omarians has expanded to such an extent, that there is to-day a desire on the part of the general reader to know something of the life of the man who gave us that "desperate sort of thing, unfortunately at the bottom of all thinking men's minds; but made music of."

MORLEY ADAMS.

HAMPSTEAD.
January, 1911.

ILLUSTRATIONS.

Edward FitzGerald's Grave	...	*Frontispiece.*	
Edward Fitzgerald's Mother	...	*To face page*	16
Bredfield White House	...	,, ,,	32
Boulge Hall	... ...	,, ,,	32
Lodgings in Market Place, Woodbridge		,, ,,	48
Little Grange	... ...	,, ,,	80
Farlingay Hall	... ...	,, ,,	80
The River Deben	... ...	,, ,,	96
The Banks of the Deben	...	,, ,,	96
Boulge Church	... ...	,, ,,	128
Boulge Cottage	... ..	,, ,,	128
Edward FitzGerald	... ...	,, ,,	144

CONTENTS.

	PAGE.
CHAPTER I.	
The FitzGerald Country	1
CHAPTER II.	
Life from 1809 to 1835	15
CHAPTER III.	
Life from 1835 to 1854	32
CHAPTER IV.	
Life from 1854 to 1874	54
CHAPTER V.	
Life from 1874 to Death in 1883 ...	74
CHAPTER VI.	
Character—Reminiscences	87
CHAPTER VII.	
Works	111
EDWARD FITZGERALD'S LETTERS	158
INDEX	173

OMAR'S INTERPRETER.

CHAPTER I.

THE FITZGERALD COUNTRY.

To THE literary man a tour of Suffolk is full of quiet delights, for it is a county not only replete with an abundance of literary associations, but boasting also of a quiet but beautiful scenery which undoubtedly contributed not a little to the inspiration of the poems of George Crabbe, Robert Bloomfield, quaint Bernard Barton, and the famous paintings of Gainsborough and Constable.

Its County Town, Ipswich, has produced no man of outstanding literary merit; it is, however, famous as the birthplace of one of the greatest characters in English history, the ambitious Cardinal Wolsey. It was intended in the reign of Henry VIII. to found Universities at Ipswich and Oxford, but the entrance gate to one of the proposed colleges is all that ever came of the scheme so far as Ipswich is concerned. However, Ipswich has its literary associations,—Charles Dickens many times walked its old-fashioned and narrow streets, and it will be remembered that it was at an Ipswich hotel that the novelist depicts

Mr. Pickwick's adventure with the lady of the yellow curl papers, while either Ipswich or Sudbury was the scene of a famous Pickwickian election.

Ipswich was also haunted by the tall, slovenly but haughty form of Edward FitzGerald, generally alone but occasionally in company with the round-faced bank clerk and Quaker poet, Bernard Barton. At other times his companion would be the son of an Ipswich corn-merchant, E. B. Cowell, who afterwards became Professor of Sanskrit at Cambridge, and who first of all introduced FitzGerald to Persian in about 1853. Cowell became the life-long friend of FitzGerald, and was indirectly the means of "Omar" being translated. Before this George Crabbe had many times visited Ipswich, and doubtless Robert Bloomfield, known as the Suffolk poet, and Thomas Wade, another minor poet, frequented the town.

The particular district, however, which represents a veritable garden of genius, starts about seven miles to the north-east of Ipswich and ends at Aldeburgh, unless, indeed, we go up into Norfolk and include the Borrow country, stately Norwich, the scene of many of his writings, and little East Dereham, his birthplace, the latter being also for many years the home of Cowper, and his friend Mrs. Unwin, who died here in 1796, her decease being followed by that of the poet himself three years later.

Woodbridge reminds one of a little lichen-covered church, one of those frequently met with in East Anglia. Quiet, ah! the beauty of that calm, and peaceful as a corner of Paradise itself. There are its narrow streets, with half-timbered houses striving to reach each other from either side of the road. They are of many dates, these houses—Tudor, Elizabethan, Renaissance, but none quite modern. Houses of many gable-ends, whole streets of them, which should bring a blush to the face of the modern motorist as he dashes through to garish Yarmouth or would-be dignified Lowestoft.

It was at Woodbridge that Bernard Barton lived the greater part of his life, and he is of peculiar interest, not only on account of his hymns and poems, but because Edward FitzGerald married his daughter Lucy.

Bernard Barton was born in 1784, in London, his mother dying in giving him birth. His stepmother sent him to a Quaker school in Ipswich. He went to Woodbridge as a coal- and corn-merchant, married and lost his wife in 1808, then went for a year as tutor to a family at Liverpool, and again returned to Woodbridge. He died in 1849, leaving a daughter Lucy.

Bernard Barton came back to Woodbridge as a bank clerk, but on more than one occasion he contemplated renouncing the bank for a literary career; Byron once remonstrated, telling him, "Do not renounce writing, but never trust entirely to authorship. If you have a profession, retain it; it will be, like Prior's Fellowship, a last and sure resource." In 1832, Charles Lamb also wrote to him, advising him to stick to the bank, "Throw yourself on the world, without any rational plan of support beyond what the chance employ of booksellers would afford you!!! Throw yourself rather, my dear sir, from the steep Tarpeian rock: slap-dash headlong upon iron spikes. If you have but five consolatory minutes between the desk and the bed, make much of them and live a century in them, rather than turn slave to the booksellers. They are Turks and Tartars when they have poor authors at their beck. Hitherto you have been at arm's length from them—come not within their grasp. . . . . Keep to the bank and the bank will keep you." Barton took the advice of his friends and kept at the bank, but he managed to publish no less than ten volumes of verse. Many of his hymns are in general use, "Walk in the Light" and "Lamp of our Feet" being, perhaps, the most familiar. FitzGerald prefixed a beautiful Memoir to his *Remains* in 1849.

To the daughter who was to become FitzGerald's wife, Barton wrote one of his sweetest sonnets. It was entitled "To My Daughter," and has been much quoted in America, if not in his native land.

"Sweet pledge of joys departed! as I lay
Wrapt in deep slumber, I beheld thee led

> By thy angelic mother, long since dead—
> Methought upon her face such smiles did play
> As gild the summer mornings. A bright ray
> Of lambent glory stream'd around her head.
> I gazed in rapture ; love had banish'd dread,
> Even as light the darkness drives away.
> Silent awhile ye stood—I could not move,
> Such sweet delight my senses did o'erpower ;
> When, in mild accents of celestial love,
> Thy guardian spoke—' Cherish this opening flower
> With holy love ; that so the future hour
> Shall reunite our souls in bliss above.' "

It was also at Woodbridge, in 1805, that Thomas Wade was born. He published in 1825 his first volume of poems, which was entitled *Tasso and the Sisters*, but if he has any claim to fame it is on account of his *Songs of the Universe and of the Heart*, which he himself called *Mundi et Cordis Carmina*, and which was published in 1835. A tragedy, "Duke Andrea," was produced with considerable success in 1828, but another, "The Jew of Arragon," was literally howled down two years later, as being too friendly to the Jews.

FitzGerald spent the most important part of his life at Woodbridge. It was here that most of his literary work was done, and a little stone tablet let into the wall of a house on Market Hill in which he lodged from 1860 to 1873, marks the spot.

On the outskirts of the little town stands " Little Grange," FitzGerald's own house, where he spent the declining years of his life. He had purchased this house against the day when he thought that he might have to leave his lodgings on the Market Hill; but even when he received notice to quit these lodgings, he felt disinclined to take up his abode at Little Grange, and took another room close to his old " home."

Little Grange is a charming old house with a beautiful garden, in which FitzGerald spent so much of his time, for Nature and his friends were the passions of his life. At Little Grange FitzGerald would only use one room, a large parlour on the ground floor, which he divided by folding doors. One part of this room was filled with books and a high writing and reading desk, and the other contained his bed. The rest of the house he furnished with great taste and left it for the use of his nieces and his visitors, among whom Charles Keene was perhaps the most frequent. He lived here the life of a hermit, for days seeing no one, unless he chanced to meet one of his nieces in the shrubbery walk of his garden, which he named the Quarterdeck, and along which he would saunter, a melancholy figure, with a plaid about his shoulders and wearing blue glasses as well as a shade over his eyes, which at this time were giving him much trouble.

About a mile and a half to the north of Woodbridge stands a fine old Jacobean mansion called Bredfield House, in which Edward

FitzGerald was born, and within a few miles are to be found Boulge Hall, where he lived for some time with his brother, and Boulge Cottage, which he turned into a sort of Bohemian den when he found it unwise to live longer with his brother at the Hall; and Farlingay Hall, where Edward lived with the owner, Mr. Job Smith, when he gave up the cottage, desiring to be still further away from his eccentric and fanatical brother John of the Hall.

Then close by is that little restful corner in which the remains of Edward FitzGerald repose beneath the roses of far Naishapur, for two bushes grown from seed brought from the tomb of Omar Khayyam have been planted upon his grave. The little churchyard of Boulge, with its ivyclad church, its huge trees, its cloister-like stillness, and its perfumes of roses and violets, whispers of ineffable peace. Year by year the rose bush blooms over the grave of FitzGerald and

" Laughing, she says, 'into the world I blow:
At once the silken Tassel of my Purse
Tear and its treasure on the Garden throw.'"

The sun dries the fallen petals and they swirl in little staccato eddies, whispering to the Hermit of Boulge in their native tongue, asking the same question as they asked of "Omar" in the long dead centuries: "Canst thou by searching find out God?"

Leaving Boulge and Woodbridge, a ride of a

few miles east brings us to quaint old-world Aldeburgh, famous as the birthplace of George Crabbe, whose works FitzGerald did so much to rescue from the oblivion into which they were fast falling. Here Crabbe first saw the light of day on the Christmas Eve of 1754. He went to school at Bungay and Stowmarket, both in Suffolk, and from 1768 to 1774 was apprenticed to a surgeon at Wickham-brook and Woodbridge. It was whilst serving his apprenticeship that he saw and fell in love with Sarah Elmy, who lived at Parham.

Upon his early struggles and seasons of dire penury, the pawning of clothing and surgical instruments, and of his appeals to Lords Thurlow, Shelburne, and North, all of which were futile, this is neither the time nor place to dwell, but no Life of FitzGerald would be complete without reference to Crabbe, for the adapter of "Omar Khayyam" became one of the closest friends of the son of the poet, and was, it is supposed, very near to becoming related in a closer sense, for at one time Edward FitzGerald was said to be in love —the phrase seems peculiar when applied to FitzGerald — with the daughter of George Crabbe (the son of the poet). No definite engagement is known to have taken place and it is thought that Caroline Crabbe was alarmed at the somewhat indefinite religious convictions of FitzGerald, and was afraid to become engaged to him. What is perhaps more probable was the fact that she was the eldest of a large family, and the duties of her father's home required her constant care and presence. Had FitzGerald married Caroline Crabbe it is doubtful whether the marriage would have been any more successful than the ill-starred alliance with Lucy Barton. FitzGerald was not the man to whom marriage was likely to bring either inspiration or happiness—but more of this anon.

Passing through Ipswich again we come to a little village called Bramford, where, after his marriage, Mr. E. B. Cowell went to reside at a charming little cottage on the banks of the river Gipping. The windows had quaint-looking red Venetian shutters. Over the front clambered a japonica and old-fashioned flowers, such as gillivers, London pride, and butter-of-witches, grew in the garden.

FitzGerald often visited the little cottage and joined Mr. and Mrs. Cowell in their studies of the Greek classics, and of Spanish and Persian. These visits to the Bramford cottage were among the happiest of FitzGerald's experiences, and he always looked back upon them with that reverence which he had for the happy past. Many years later, after the Cowells had left Bramford, FitzGerald, writing to Mr. Cowell from Woodbridge, reminds him of the happy Bramford days, of the church, river, fields and woods, and describes it as a haunt of ancient peace, and the retrospect made him sad at heart, for the days were no more.

Going towards Bury St. Edmunds we come to a small village called Honington, where in 1776, Robert Bloomfield was born. His father was a tailor and died while the poet was a child, and at eleven years of age he was placed with his uncle, a struggling farmer, with whom it was intended that he should learn farming, but being too diminutive for farm-labour he was sent to London to learn the trade of a shoemaker. However, his country training supplied material for his "Farmer's Boy," and gave a rugged reality to his writings.

After the manuscript of "The Farmer's Boy" had been rejected by many London editors, young Bloomfield showed it to a Captain Lofft, a Suffolk literary lawyer and squire. He recognised its originality and rough beauty. He introduced it to the world, and the work straightway became popular, being translated into French, Italian, and parts of it even into Latin. No less than 26,000 copies were sold in less than three years. Other works by Bloomfield which gained more or less notice are "Rural Tales," "The Banks of the Wye," "The Soldier's Home," which Christopher North described as no whit inferior to Burns' "Soldier's Return," and "May-day with the Muses." He took to many occupations, among others the making of Æolian harps, and bookselling, but was notably unfortunate. The latter part of his life, when half-blind and suffering from intense irritability, wellnigh to madness, was spent at Shefford, in Bedfordshire. For the works of Bloomfield FitzGerald had much admiration, but his friend Charles Lamb found "The Farmer's Boy" unappetising.

Not a great way from Honington is Merton Rectory, to which on the 13th of June, 1883, FitzGerald set off, never to return alive. On the day previous to his departure he wrote to his friend Laurence, the last letter that he, who was a Prince of letter writers, ever wrote.

A reference to Bury St. Edmunds should also be made in describing the FitzGerald country. He went to Merton Rectory on his last journey *via* Bury to see the school. The claim that Bury St. Edmunds has to literary distinction is the fact that it is the birthplace of Ouida, who was born there about the year 1840, and who in spite of her French name (Mdlle. de lá Ramée) comes on her father's side from Suffolk farming stock. Though Ouida is amazingly inaccurate in matters of every-day observation, and though her characters are generally conventional and her ideals invariably tawdry and unwholesome, her stories have delighted hundreds of readers, and Suffolk is proud to name her among its *literati*. It was at Bury St. Edmunds that FitzGerald went to school after he left the private school at Woodbridge, where he received the rudiments of his education. He joined his elder brother, John, at King Edward's School, Bury, in 1821. It was here that he made many friends—friendships to be severed only by death. Tom Spedding and his brother James, W. Bodham Donne, J. M. Kemble ("Anglo-Saxon" Kemble), were among those of his Bury schoolfellows. Thus Bury St. Edmunds, which played an important part in the lives of Goldsmith and Defoe, also influenced Edward FitzGerald.

A visit ought certainly to be paid to quaint old Reydon Hall, where in 1796, Miss Agnes Strickland was born. She, together with her sister Elizabeth, wrote that copious and elaborate *Lives of the Queens of England*, with its vivid pictures of English court life. Agnes Strickland began writing early in life, and turned out a prodigious amount of work. Her first work was a series of historic stories for children, called *Worcester Field, or the Cavalier*, followed in 1835 by *The Pilgrims of Walsingham*, after the style of Chaucer's *Canterbury Pilgrims*. Among other works were *Lives of the Tudor Princesses, Lives of the Seven Bishops*, and *Bachelor Kings of England*.

Our literary survey of Suffolk must now end, though the subject is not by any means exhausted. Much might be said of Sudbury, the birthplace of the immortal Gainsborough, and delightful little East Bergholt, where another painter of equal merit, the great Constable, first saw the light of day.

Again, it would be pleasant to dwell upon the associations of the literary salon of Mrs. Biddell of Playford, where the local literary folk foregathered to talk "books" and evolve epigrams over dinner, which was purposely prolonged to extend from three in the afternoon to nine in the evening. Here Mrs. Biddell, Miss Charlesworth (afterwards Professor Cowell's wife), Edward FitzGerald, Mrs. Fulcher, and G. W. Fulcher (known locally as the Crabbe of Sudbury), and occasionally Robert Southey, met and compared poems and literary compositions.

Then mention should be made of Saxmundham, the home of Mitford, editor of *Gray*, and for many years editor of the *Gentleman's Magazine;* and historical Framlingham of Bigod fame, where an intimate friend of FitzGerald's, Archdeacon Groome, was born, but FitzGerald became intimate with him whilst he was Rector of Monk Soham. And so one might go on, for literary associations of the district come crowding into one's mind, and one would fain give them expression.

That the district was dear to the heart of FitzGerald, a glance through his letters will prove. He loved its quiet solitude, its cowslip-besprinkled meadows, its leafy lanes, and, above all, its rambling rivers and lake-like estuaries.

It called to him like the frozen North calls to the explorer who has once visited its icy fastnesses.

On one occasion FitzGerald started on his yacht, the " Scandal," to make a trip to Holland. They sailed down the beautiful Deben and out at its mouth at Bawdsey into the open sea. The wind was contrary all the time, but at last the shores of Holland were seen in the distance. His captain happened to remark that there was a better wind backwards than forwards, whereupon FitzGerald ordered him to turn the yacht towards the English coast, and back they went to Woodbridge, for Woodbridge was calling him and he must go.

CHAPTER II.

LIFE FROM 1809 TO 1835.

IT is not my intention to write much in the nature of a FitzGerald biography. This has been more or less ably done by A. C. Benson, Thomas Wright, John Glyde and by Francis Hindes Groome in his delightful little silhouette entitled "Two Suffolk Friends." Therefore little remains to be told, but I have so often followed in the footsteps of Edward FitzGerald at Woodbridge, Bredfield and Boulge, and less frequently at Bury, Cambridge and Bedford, that I have managed to gather some information —mostly in the way of little human touches— that has been overlooked by other biographers.

Edward FitzGerald was born at the White House, Bredfield, Suffolk, on March 31st, 1809, and was the third son of John and Mary Frances Purcell, of Irish descent and first cousins. Edward FitzGerald's father, Mr. John Purcell, upon the death of his wife's father in 1818, took to himself the FitzGerald name and arms and was afterwards known as John Purcell FitzGerald. He is described as a big, powerful, ruddy-faced man of kindly disposition, impulsive and inclined to be too credulous. He was, however, almost a nonentity, being entirely overshadowed by the magnificent Mrs. FitzGerald, Edward's mother.

It was from his mother that the boy derived his force of character, and inherited his mental power together with a certain amount of eccentricity, doubtless accentuated by the intermarriage of cousins.

Mrs. FitzGerald was beautiful, dazzlingly so, gifted and well educated. She revelled in Art and Poetry, spoke four languages and was exceedingly well read. Her beauty is said to have been exquisite, almost ethereal; an oval face, perfect, but not monotonous features, magnificent dark eyes full of lurid fire, a wealth of luxuriant dark hair, which Poe would have described as "hyacinthine," somewhat haughty of mien as became the woman whose beauty is said to have dazzled kings. She inspired in the breasts of her children a feeling of awesome admiration rather than love, and from her visits to the nursery they derived little comfort. Edward, years afterwards, remarked, when relating how he had caught a boy up one of his walnut trees, "He was as scared as I was when my own mother came to see me at Bredfield nursery."

Edward was the seventh child, Mary Frances, John, Andalusia, Mary Eleanor, Jane and Peter being born prior to his advent and Isabella after it. Of the brothers and sisters of Edward FitzGerald, it will be necessary for me to occasionally refer to the second child, John,

THE MOTHER OF EDWARD FITZGERALD.

whose life was largely interwoven with that of his brother Edward.

Edward FitzGerald used to say, "We (the FitzGeralds) are all mad, but with this difference, *I* know that I am." John was the maddest of them all. I have have been told numerous anecdotes by Woodbridge folk who knew him well, that go far to confirm the supposition. On one occasion a Woodbridge tradesman received an order from John FitzGerald—then living at Boulge—for a carpet to be supplied and laid in one of his rooms. It was particularly intimated that the tradesman should personally fit the carpet to the room. In due time it was brought, and the furnisher took an assistant to help him in the fitting. John FitzGerald, for some inexplicable reason, resented the presence of the third man, and looked at the poor assistant with considerable displeasure and then left the room. The carpet was laid and Mr. John called in, and asked if it was satisfactory. Without even looking at it, he frowned, and in reply to the query, "Will it do, sir?" he snapped out—"No, it won't do! Roll it up and take it back again!"

Knowing the idiosyncrasies of his customer, the tradesman sent his assistant home and himself pottered about for half an hour, when Mr. John FitzGerald again came into the room. He beamed down upon the carpet and then said in his usual deliberate way of speaking, which on account of a slight impediment seemed to fairly scintillate with S's—" Yes—that—will—do—very nicely—*very*—nicely indeed."

Like his brother Edward, John FitzGerald appeared to be always preoccupied when walking, and would keenly resent any interruption of his reverie. On more than one occasion he strode into the " Bull " at Woodbridge and gave orders for a carriage and pair to take him to Boulge. He would give his order and then walk on, telling the coachman to overtake him. He was an exceptionally quick walker, and often he would arrive almost at Boulge before the conveyance overtook him.

" I 'ud drive just behind 'un," said the coachman in telling the story, " and he 'ud walk on with one of his moods on 'im; I darn't interrupt 'im—I did unce and he jawed me for half-an-hour—so I 'ud whistle and cough, but bless yer it wasn't no use ; once I blowed a horn and he jest looked up as if a starlin' was a'singin'."

When the bill for the conveyance was sent in, he would point out that he was charged for occasions on which he did not have a carriage, but after the lapse of a few days the account would always be paid in full.

John FitzGerald had a passion for what Edward called " Religion," which almost amounted to dementia. He prepared himself for the Church, which it was his ambition to enter. A severe fever, however, so affected his eyes and nerves that he had to abandon his ambition, but until the time of his death he never missed an opportunity of preaching, and even in the pulpit his eccentricities displayed themselves. On one occasion at the Bunyan Meeting House, Bedford, when a member of the congregation, he waited until the preacher, the Rev. John Jukes, entered the pulpit and then started to undress himself. He removed his boots and stockings and several other small articles of attire, and emptied his pockets, putting their contents on the seat by his side.

John FitzGerald was an intimate friend and colleague of the Rev. T. R. Matthews, of the well-known "Matthews' Chapel," Bromham Road, Bedford. Edward never "took kindly" to his brother, and always kept as far away from him as possible.

A letter which Edward FitzGerald wrote to Robert Hindes Groome, containing a mildly humorous reference to his brother John, dwells upon his eccentricities, and advises Groome never to take it to heart if his brother disappointed him in not keeping appointments. Edward told him to leave meetings to chance, and thus save poor John an immense deal of "taking the Lord's name in vain." John Fitz-Gerald's eternal D.V., Edward points out, means, "If I happen to be in the humour"; feeling *bound* to keep an appointment was just the reason he would not keep it, which Edward points out was rather the case with himself and he therefore rarely made appointments.

Edward spent his early days in the White House at Bredfield, and in the delightful park and woods that surrounded it. Bredfield House (as it is now called) is a charming old Jacobean mansion, which can be seen through the trees from the road. It is encased in white plaster, from which fact it evidently derived its name. The rooms are to-day much as they were when the infant Edward lived there. The nursery where the children played, and where they were periodically visited and awed by the imperial Mrs. FitzGerald, is much as it then was and the " Magistrates' room," in which Edward " used to be whipped," and in which the neighbouring gentry, many of them magistrates, used to meet, and, over pipe and punch-bowl, talk over the day's fox-hunting, remains unaltered. The shrubs in front of the house, behind which Edward was wont to hide to see his mother's coach " of a good, full yellow colour," start on its journey to the town residence of the FitzGeralds in Portland Place, have, however, disappeared. In addition to Bredfield House and the mansion in Portland Place, the FitzGeralds had a Manor-house at Naseby—often visited by the youthful Edward —a fine house at Seaford and another at Castle Irwell, Manchester. They collected pictures— a trait inherited by Edward—and owned some

magnificent gold plate, which is said to have
"dazzled the eyes of the less fortunate," and a
set of ground glass and burnished silver, the like
of which did not exist in the country, if indeed
in the whole world.

His father spent money lavishly, his stable
was second to none in the county, and his
shooting was the envy of his neighbours, but
he had no business ability and his wealth—
great as it was—was swallowed up by his wild
speculation in digging for coal on his Manchester
estate.

At five years of age, Edward was taken by his
father to Paris, and much time was spent there
by the boy in each of the next few years.

In after years Edward FitzGerald dwelt
lovingly on the early days of Bredfield Hall; the
past was always a passion with him and the
lapse of years only gave an added lustre. It
was evidently Bredfield, with its profusion of
flowers that inspired his beautiful little poem,
written in 1831, called "The Meadows in
Spring," and it was the memories of these days
that caused him to write those charming
stanzas entitled "Bredfield Hall." This poem
is one of the finest of his purely original
works, and I have reproduced it in the chapter
headed "Writings." Everyone may obtain
the immortal "Omar"—it can be bought
complete for, one penny—but "Bredfield Hall"
is less known and not so readily obtained. For

some time Edward attended a private school in Woodbridge—the building is still standing, and in 1821, being then just over twelve years old, he joined his brother John at King Edward's School at Bury St. Edmunds. The school had a high reputation, its pupils carrying off many of the Cambridge classical prizes. Special attention was given to the writing of English, and a more suitable school for the embryo writer—whose forte was surely English—could not have been found. The FitzGeralds left Bredfield House in 1825 and moved to Wherstead Lodge, near Ipswich, which had previously been in the possession of Lord Granville.

Wherstead Lodge, the home of the FitzGeralds for ten years, is a very charming house standing close to the mouth of the noble Orwell. To Wherstead Edward came for his vacation, and he was often to be seen in Ipswich poring over volumes in the bookshops, especially the bookshop of Mr. James Ried.

On February 6th, 1826, Edward was entered at Trinity College, Cambridge, and obtained lodgings at a Mrs. Perry's, 19, King's Parade.

The Master of Trinity at that time was Christopher Wordsworth, the youngest brother of the poet. One of the tutors was the future Dean Peacock and another, Connop Thirlwall, became in later years Bishop of St. Davids.

It was at Trinity that FitzGerald made some

of his closest friends, chief among whom was William Makepeace Thackeray, who went to Cambridge in 1829, another was W. H. Thompson, who afterwards became Master of Trinity, others being John M. Kemble, James Spedding, the celebrated Parliamentarian, Frederick Maurice, and Charles Buller.

Two of FitzGerald's greatest friends, both of whom left a considerable name in literature and one of whom became Laureate, were Frederick and Alfred Tennyson, his contemporaries at Cambridge, but it was some time after the Cambridge days that the acquaintance which ripened into so warm and close a friendship began. For FitzGerald to make a friend was to keep him—like the past, and the sea and all nature, friendships were with him passions, and only to be relinquished as " Destiny with men for pieces plays " and " one by one back in the closet lays."

At Cambridge FitzGerald was not a devoted student, he dallied with his studies, read voraciously, mostly the classical authors, painted in water-colour, and occupied himself with poetry and music. His time passed pleasantly enough with his friends, his pipe, coffee, songs, and sketches. His parents kept him well supplied with money, which he seemed to spend on everything except clothes. In this respect he was one of the most untidy men at the college, and all through his life he cared nothing for his personal appearance. His magnificent mother used occasionally to visit him at Cambridge, and the contrast between the two was striking. Mrs. FitzGerald would drive up like a queen in her magnificent yellow coach, drawn by four coal-black horses. She would be arrayed in the most costly and choicest of purple and fine linen, and peerless in her beauty. Her son Edward—well, some idea of the state of his wardrobe may be gained by the fact that on one of his mother's visits Edward sent back word by the man-servant that he had no boots in which to come. He finally did answer the summons, and walked round Cambridge with his mother, but it was in somebody else's boots! This I learned from an old man in Boulge, who often "had a few words with Master Edward." He, knowing Edward FitzGerald's generosity, upon one occasion asked "Master Edward" for a pair of boots. "You don't want boots," said FitzGerald, half in jest, half in earnest. "Walk about without them or borrow some, I had no boots when I walked about Cambridge with my mother. I borrowed some." One cannot help wondering from whom he borrowed them! Surely from one of his friends, perhaps from the future Dean of Lincoln, or from Richard Monckton-Milnes, afterwards Lord Houghton!

FitzGerald managed to take a degree in 1830, and then began that vague, hermit-like existence, which ended at Merton Rectory fifty-three years later.

After leaving Cambridge, FitzGerald went on a visit to his sister Eleanor, who had married a Mr. Kerrick, at Geldestone Hall, near Beccles, a delightful little town on the Waveney. A town of quaint streets, with an old-world beauty about it—a town beloved by FitzGerald except for its name, which he said reminded him of hooks and eyes. It was at Beccles that the poet Crabbe was nearly drowned, owing to the capsizing of a boat in which he was taking his sweetheart (Sarah Elmy, " Mira ") for a row on the Waveney. Mrs. Kerrick—FitzGerald's favourite sister—he describes as a clever person, fond of literary pursuits, absent, careless, fond of educating and giving advice. FitzGerald made many friends at Beccles, chief of whom were Dr. Edward Crowfoot, and later on in life, Mr. W. Aldis Wright.

The same year (1830) FitzGerald stayed with his Aunt Purcell in Paris, and as his friend Thackeray was also in that city, they spent much time together. Many happy mornings were spent at the Louvre, where Thackeray was supposed to be studying Art. The friends walked about the Boulevards, and on one occasion FitzGerald stopped by the Madeleine to listen to a street singer. Several onlookers joined in the song, and FitzGerald, having purchased a copy of the words, assisted in the singing, as he says in a letter to Fanny Kemble: " I joined in the words, which the man called out beforehand (as they do hymns in church)."

It is supposed by some that this visit of FitzGerald to Paris was a clandestine one, he having secretly arranged to meet Thackeray there beforehand, as he had told his tutor that he was to spend his vacation in Huntingdonshire.

From Paris FitzGerald crossed to Southampton, whilst Thackeray went to Germany. He was joined at Southampton by his friend John Allen, who was staying at Portsmouth. He walked over from that town to see FitzGerald, but arriving late at night found that he had retired to bed.

Relating the incident Allen says: "Got up and went to FitzGerald's room, who jumped up and almost cried for joy to see me, dear affectionate fellow! After breakfast, though very stiff, walked with him to Netley Abbey, and tried to make him steady in his views on religion."

After this FitzGerald went to his father's estate at Naseby, where he lodged in a delightful old farm-house and spent a quietly happy time, writing poems, and gossiping with the simple country folk (a pastime he ever loved). It was during this stay at Naseby that he wrote the very sweet little lyric with its original metre "The Meadows in Spring," which will be found in the chapter "Writings." The poem is delightful for many reasons—there is a beautiful though melancholy sentiment in its retrospect, and the echoes of the last line of each stanza are exceedingly tuneful. In it is displayed much of the genius of Edward FitzGerald—his genius of construction, euphony and contrast. The poem appeared in 1831 in Hone's *Year Book* and in the *Athenæum* on July 9th of the same year. It was published anonymously and was credited by many to Charles Lamb, who says of it, "'Tis a poem I envy—that and Montgomery's 'Last Man'—I envy the writers because I feel that I could have done something like them."

Back again at Bredfield, FitzGerald delights himself among the roses—what a subtle part roses played in FitzGerald's life—with his painting, writing and music. He makes friends of the people in the neighbourhood, especially Perry Nursey of Little Bealings and Robert Newton Shawe of Kosgrave Hall.

FitzGerald visited Lowestoft in 1831, where he delighted to stroll across the Denes or along the shore. He loved the sea, it was one of his passions, and it is not emphasised half enough in any of the biographies that have been written, unless indeed it be in *Two Suffolk Friends*, which can scarcely be called a biography. His letters are full of it: a slice—a very large slice—of his life was spent on it. His "Sea-Words and Phrases along the Suffolk Coast," which appeared in the *East Anglian Daily Times* in 1868-9, is among the most delightful of his works. Several

of these are quoted in *Two Suffolk Friends.*
I give three:

"*Bark.*—'The surf *bark* from the Nor'ard' or, as was otherwise said to me, 'The sea ain't lost his woice from the Nor'ard yet'—a sign, by the way, that the wind is to come from that quarter. A poetical word such as those whose business is with the sea are apt to use. Listening one night to the sea some way inland, a sailor said to me, 'Yes, sir, the sea roar for the loss of the wind': which a landsman properly interpreted as meaning only that the sea made itself heard when the wind had subsided."

"*Egg-bound.*—Probably an inland word; but it was only from one of the beach that I heard it. He had a pair of—what does the reader think?—turtle-doves in his net-loft, looking down so drolly—the delicate creatures—from their wicker cage on the rough work below, that I wondered what business they had there. But this truculent Salwager assured me seriously that he had 'doated on them,' and promised me the first pair they should hatch. For a long while they had no family, so long '*neutral*,' indeed, as to cause grave doubts whether they were a pair at all. But at last one of them began to show signs of cradle-making, picking at some hay stuffed into the wicker-bars to encourage them; and I was told that she was manifestly '*egg-bound.*'"

"*Cards.*—Though often carried on board to

pass away the time at All-fours, Don, or Sir-wiser (q.v.), nevertheless regarded with some suspicion when business does not go right. A friend of mine vowed that, if his ill-luck continued, over the cards should go; and over they went. Opinions differ as to swearing. One captain strictly forbade it on board his lugger; but he, also continuing to get no fish, called out: 'Swear away, lads, and see what that'll do!' Perhaps he only meant as Ménage's French bishop did; who, going one day to Court, his carriage stuck fast in the slough. The coachman swore; the bishop put his head out of the window, and asked him not to do that; the coachman declared that unless he did, his horses would never get the carriage out of the mud. 'Well, then,' says the bishop, 'just for this once then.'"

In sailors and fishermen, and all things nautical, FitzGerald always took a keen interest and, as will be shewn hereafter, he made a friend and even an idol of one fisherman.

In the following year, 1832, George Crabbe, the poet in whose life and works FitzGerald took such a keen interest, died, on February 3rd.

About this time FitzGerald wrote his poem "To a Lady Singing," a beautiful fragment with a haunting melody. It is thought by some that the "Clora" of the poem was Anne Allen, and the fanciful idea of the lost chord being followed and found by the singer—if indeed

Anne Allen was meant—was soon fulfilled, for she died soon after. In the poem he asks if Clora can tell whither the sweet song sang into the wild summer air, falleth or flieth, and the most beautiful verse answers the question—

> "Melody, dying away
>   Into the dark sky, closes
> Like the good soul from his clay,
>   Like the fair odour of roses,
> Therefore thou now art behind it,
> But thou shalt follow and find it."

In February, 1833, we find FitzGerald staying at his father's Manchester seat, Castle Irwell— the fatal spot that afterwards swallowed so relentlessly all his father's vast wealth and a large portion of that of his friend and neighbour jovial old Squire Jenny. In September he is in lodgings in London, near the British Museum, and often sees Spedding, Thackeray, and Tennyson. They frequently met at "The Cock," in Fleet Street, where Browne occasionally joined them, and the time passed very pleasantly. The greater part of 1833 was spent at the British Museum, poring over and copying numerous manuscripts.

In November of this year there came to FitzGerald the news of the death of his friend Anne Allen, at the early age of twenty-five. The loss was deeply mourned by FitzGerald, who wrote in memory of her the touching lines which take their title from her name.

In 1834 he went to stay with the Brownes at Bedford, and until Browne's marriage in 1844, he made the visits an annual institution. The friends devoted much time to riding, shooting, and fishing, and FitzGerald then and afterwards "was in love with Bedfordshire." The next year he is visiting Spedding at Mirehouse, on Bassenthwaite Lake, by Skiddaw, where he amused himself by sketching and playing chess with Spedding's mother. Alfred Tennyson came on a visit at the same time, and with him FitzGerald spent many happy hours.

Some years before, FitzGerald's father had purchased Boulge Hall, not far from Bredfield House, subject to the life interest of Mrs. Short, who resided there. This lady now being dead, the FitzGeralds decide to make this their home, and after a residence of ten years at Wherstead, a sad farewell was taken of it, and the family moved to Boulge Hall in 1835.

CHAPTER III.

LIFE FROM 1835 TO 1854.

BOULGE HALL, is a large house of the Queen Anne style, with a large and beautiful garden, which, however, FitzGerald describes as one of the ugliest and dullest places in England.

Whatever Boulge may have been in the early days of FitzGerald, it is to-day one of the loveliest and most restful spots in the country. Rich pastures, covered with cowslips, primrose bedecked copses, the old-world flint church with its warm brick tower, in the shadow of which Edward FitzGerald reposes, and hard by the peaceful river Deben—so beloved by him— these make up a scene of quiet sylvan beauty which soothes and enchants.

Almost at the same time that the family took up their residence at Boulge, the living of Bredfield became vacant, and George Crabbe, son of the poet, was appointed to it. George Crabbe, now Vicar of Bredfield, and a great friend of the FitzGerald family, was a strong, powerful man, bluff, lovable, impetuous and rash. His daughters used to take all the money from his pockets before he left the house, for fear none would be left when he returned.

BREDFIELD WHITE HOUSE.
(Edward FitzGerald's birthplace.)

Photo. Welton, Woodbridge.

BOULGE HALL, WOODBRIDGE.

Photo. Welton, Woodbridge.

He was greatly beloved by all in the parish and in return he loved and prayed for them all, including "Mary Ann Cuthbert, the only black sheep in his flock." He was a man of much talent, and his *Life* of his father, written in 1835, has become a classic. FitzGerald himself declared it to be "one of the most delightful memoirs in the language." He was a Bohemian of the Bohemians, and used to sit in his horrible little den reeking with tobacco smoke and smelling like the parlour of an inn. FitzGerald always referred to this den as "the Cobblery," and it was a place after his own heart.

The Vicarage was to the FitzGeralds as much their home as was Boulge Hall. They— especially Edward—went in and out as they pleased, and it is said, as already mentioned, that FitzGerald fell in love with the eldest Miss Crabbe, Caroline Matilda, but this must not be accepted as final, indeed it is strongly denied by many living friends of FitzGerald, including Mr. John Loder of Woodbridge and the lady's maid of the Crabbes. These, one would think, would probably have known had such been the case.

In January, 1837, FitzGerald pays another visit to Geldestone Hall, where he makes friends —as he usually did—with an old lady named Mrs. Schutz, and is delighted with her conversation and agreeable manners.

Returning to Boulge, he had a desire to have

a den of his own, inspired, doubtless, by Crabbe's "Cobblery," and he decided to take up his abode in a little thatched cottage at the gates of Boulge Park.

To a man of simple tastes such as FitzGerald, this little picturesque thatched cottage, offered a real home. It was in keeping with its tenant, and one can better picture him enjoying his Bohemian disposition here than in the mansions of Bredfield, Portland Place or Naseby. To him for sixteen years it proved "Paradise enow," and perhaps the most interesting period of his life was spent in this little Boulge Cottage.

It is a building of but two apartments, with no "upstairs." FitzGerald made the room on the right his study, den, "cobblery," and that on the left his bedroom. In the dwelling at the back—really a part of the cottage—dwelt an old Waterloo man, named John Faire, and his wife. The latter, "a snuffy but vain old woman," looked after "Mr. Edward." John Faire was esteemed by FitzGerald on account of being a Waterloo man, who had fought in the great battle and guarded Napoleon at St. Helena. In the campaign he lost a thumb, but, as he pointed out, another man in the village had three thumbs, which adjusted matters.

FitzGerald's "den" presented a strange appearance, a conglomeration, among which might be distinguished a bust of Shakespeare in a recess, a cat on the hearth-rug, a dog, a parrot named "Beauty Bob," a piano piled high with books, music, and MSS., in hopeless confusion, a barrel of beer, and the Man himself.

In a letter to his friend Allen he pictures his life in the cottage, surely an "Omar"-like existence. He pointed out that he lived with tolerable content, all the morning reading about Nero in Tacitus, and lying on a bench in the garden. He talks about the singing of nightingales and the blooming of gay flowers. He lunches at one on Cambridge cream-cheese, and in the afternoon rides over hill and dale and does some gardening. His simple life is one of contentment and happiness, the chatting of a little girl, his sister's child, gives him infinite pleasure. These simple country joys make up a life which he loves, and he always looked back upon these days as among his happiest.

Here in his little cottage with the window open—in the daytime to let in the sweet odours of roses and cowslips, and at night to let out the tobacco smoke,—FitzGerald would sit in dressing-gown and slippers, pipe in mouth, and muse, the thoughtful soul retired to solitude.

A Woodbridge man brought him his letters and shaved him three times a week, and the monotony would be broken by occasional visits to church on Sundays.

For some time FitzGerald had known and become interested in Bernard Barton the poet, and about this time (1838) they became fast friends, and some of the letters written to him by FitzGerald are among the best that he ever penned. He also corresponded with Frederick Tennyson whilst at the cottage. In one of his letters he tells of the joy of returning to the country after a sojourn in London, and we can almost smell the China roses climbing up the windows. Here he found the heart of England beating healthily, and his afternoon rides would occasionally be varied by a walk with a great black dog, and the evenings spent beside the open windows, in which the roses climbed, listening to the blackbirds and thrushes rustling bedwards. He describes the coming spring, the bursting of the oaks into leaf and the grass striving with the buttercups. "How old to tell of, how new to see."

From the Boulge Cottage FitzGerald would make various excursions into the country and occasionally to London. On one of these London visits he went for a drive with Dickens, Thackeray and Tennyson. On another occasion he, in the company of Tennyson, visited Stratford-on-Avon, where he was more moved by the sight of the footpath so often trodden by Shakespeare than by his house or tomb—just what we should have expected of FitzGerald.

Now (1842) begins his friendship with Carlyle. In company with Dr. Arnold, Carlyle had visited the battlefield of Naseby and seen the obelisk which FitzGerald's father had erected, not to commemorate the scene of the battle, as they thought, but to mark the highest ground. Together with Thackeray, FitzGerald called upon Carlyle and enlightened him as to the real object of the Naseby obelisk. FitzGerald himself made some excavations at Naseby and found a large number of skeletons packed closely together, and he many times spoke of marking the spot by a granite slab, but this was never done. However, the incident did much to ripen the acquaintance of Carlyle and FitzGerald into friendship which lasted until the death of the former in 1881.

In July, 1843, FitzGerald paid a visit to Ireland—he had been there twice before. He stayed at an Hotel in Dublin, where he was considerably inconvenienced by being locked in the bathroom, accidentally, with a bath full of scalding hot water. He visited his Uncle Peter at Kilcullen and wrote a prologue to one of Calderon's plays for his cousins who were giving some private theatricals, and he went on various explorations.

Returning to Boulge he resumes his old quiet life, visits Crabbe, takes tea with Bernard Barton, and strolls over to Hasketon to talk with Squire Jenny.

During his annual visits to Bedford FitzGerald saw much of the Rev. T. R. Matthews, a popular evangelical preacher and the idol of John FitzGerald. On the night of Good Friday,

1844, Edward FitzGerald gathered with a huge crowd in front of the Bromham Road Chapel, and as soon as the doors were open, crowded into the building. FitzGerald sat in the far end of the chapel, close to the pulpit. Matthews, a big man with aquiline nose and prominent eyebrows, and hair which fell over his neck and then curled upwards, preached a wonderful sermon on the Crucifixion with such fervour that people were moved to tears, and when Matthews earnestly entreated that some of his hearers would express their belief in Christ, almost all rose to their feet. "I was quite overset," says FitzGerald; "all poor people: how much richer than all who fill the London churches."

This experience is worth relating because it was the only time that FitzGerald was impressed by preaching, a thing that he largely held in mild contempt.

This year is marked by the marriage of FitzGerald's great Bedford friend, Browne, and with much foreboding FitzGerald thought that he must for ever bid farewell to the happy Bedford days. But the Brownes settled down at Goldington Hall, just to the north of Bedford, and FitzGerald was to spend many more happy days with his dearest friend.

The next year Matthews died suddenly in his apartments under Bromham Road Chapel, and Edward and John FitzGerald attended the funeral. On the following Sunday John FitzGerald delivered a funeral address in the chapel, and for some time continued as nominal pastor of the Church.

In the following year FitzGerald formed another great friendship—a friendship that was to have far-reaching results, and the outcome of which was immortality to one of them. This friend was E. B. Cowell, afterwards professor of Sanskrit at Cambridge. Cowell, the son of an Ipswich tradesman, was at this time twenty years of age. He took to books quite early in life and voraciously devoured those that he obtained from the Ipswich Institute library. His father gave him a copy of the *Edinburgh Review* which contained Macaulay's article on Warren Hastings. In the end of the magazine was an advertisement in the form of a book list which included *An Introduction to the Grammar of the Sanskrit Language, for the use of early students*, by H. H. Wilson, M.A. Wrapped up in that advertisement was FitzGerald's immortality! The boy Cowell saved up his pocket money and bought the book at Christmas.

In after years it was Cowell who introduced Persian to FitzGerald, and but for that introduction he would never have learnt the language and never have translated "Omar."

E. B. Cowell it was who married the Miss Charlesworth, mentioned in Chapter I. Cowell was a modest, shy, simple-minded man, a devout student of the Bible and deeply religious. In after years he half regretted that he had been the means of introducing Persian to FitzGerald—"Omar," a poem of Doubt, beautiful as poetry, was contrary to the all trustful faith of Cowell, and years after "Omar" was translated he wrote: "I unwittingly incurred a grave responsibility when I introduced his poems to my old friend in 1856. I admire Omar as I admire Lucretius, but I cannot take him as a guide. In these grave matters I prefer to go to Nazareth, not to Naishapur."

As I before pointed out, FitzGerald was a constant visitor to Cowell, who had married and settled at the cottage at Bramford, and here they all studied Persian together, and the days were to FitzGerald a delicious dream. After Cowell had gone up to Oxford—which FitzGerald moved heaven and earth to prevent—in a letter to the Vicar of Bredfield, he remarks how he is saddened at the thoughts of Bramford forsaken and all desolate, and how he would have to turn away his head whenever the spire of the little church came into view. He wrote many letters to the Cowells "abusing" them, as he says, for going to Oxford.

FitzGerald was still living—when at home—in Boulge Cottage, and he spent his days in thinking much and writing little. He would occasionally go to the village school at both

Bredfield and Debach and teach the children. At the latter place he taught the elder scholars the theory of music from the blackboard by a method of his own. The children took to music with great readiness but were much embarrassed when striving, under FitzGerald's tuition, to pronounce the names of the surrounding villages. " Debach " said FitzGerald, " is spoken just as it is spelt with a little ' De ' and a big ' bach '—do not call it ' Debidge,' which is not pretty, too much like cabbage, and Boulge, isn't Bulge: call it ' Boolge.' " He also experienced considerable difficulty in getting them to pronounce the final g's—a Suffolk failing—" Why do you call it ' Beal*ins*,' " he asked, " it's Beal*ings*," and when " er " came at the end of a word Suffolk children would—and will—pronounce it as " a." Butter was always " butta " and master " masta," and the patient FitzGerald would spend hours in helping them to master the difficulties.

This information I obtained from an old gentleman at Boulge who was in one of the classes which FitzGerald taught. He also related to me an incident which has never before been published and which shews that FitzGerald was a man of generous impulses, though in the present instance it was perilously near to " compounding a felony." The boy—now the man relating the incident—watched FitzGerald leave Boulge Cottage and walk towards Woodbridge. Such an opportunity was not to be missed.

At the back of the cottage grew a fine walnut tree, with walnuts just fit for gathering. Stealing in at the Park Gates the boy started to throw stones and sticks at the heavily laden tree and to fill his pockets with walnuts. Presently a large dog appeared upon the scene, followed by the form of FitzGerald himself. Blazing with a righteous indignation, but restraining it, FitzGerald approached the lad and said:

"Have you ever heard that—

"A dog, a woman, and a walnut tree,
The more you beat them the better they be."

"I thought," said the man, relating the incident, "that it was a text from the Scriptures and answered that I had heard Parson Crabbe say it." "Well," answered FitzGerald, "it's quite true but I do not want my walnut tree to be any better than it is. But the saying also applies to boys," and FitzGerald administered a well-earned chastisement, whilst the boy roared with fright rather than pain. Directly he had seen FitzGerald the lad had emptied his pockets of the walnuts, which were now lying on the ground. Still weeping, the boy started for home, when FitzGerald called him back and asked him why he was leaving the walnuts to waste on the ground, and told him to fill his pockets again. After this was done for some unknown reason — unless it was remorse —

FitzGerald gave him half-a-crown and sent him home smiling.

At the Bredfield School a Mrs. Jasper was mistress and Miss Caroline Crabbe went at intervals to assist. FitzGerald was often to be seen after the school hours were over, accompanying Miss Crabbe to the vicarage.

In 1849, FitzGerald experienced a serious blow, by the death of his poet friend, whom he had grown to dearly love, Bernard Barton. For some time the latter's health had been failing, but he continued to attend to his duties at the bank and almost up to the last he formed one of the company which met at the cottage at Boulge with Crabbe and Thomas Churchyard, where with FitzGerald they would sit and smoke and talk literature and village politics. FitzGerald dubbed them the "Wits of Woodbridge."

On the 19th of February, Barton was unable to get to the bank, and spent the day on his sofa. He retired to bed early and suddenly rang his bell. His daughter answered the summons and reached his side just before he breathed his last.

On February 24th, 1849, FitzGerald contributed a column, containing an appreciation of the dead poet, to the *Ipswich Journal* (since deceased). After considerable difficulty I managed to obtain a copy of the *Journal* of that date and from it I have taken FitzGerald's report.

Death of Bernard Barton.

"At Woodbridge, on the night of Monday last, February 19th, between the hours of 8 and 9, after a brief spasm in the heart, died Bernard Barton. He was born near London in 1784, came to Woodbridge in 1806, where he shortly after married, and was left a widower at the birth of his only child, who now survives him. In 1810 he entered as clerk in Messrs. Alexander's Bank, where he officiated almost to the day of his death. He had been for some months afflicted with laborious breathing, which his doctor knew to proceed from disease in the heart; though there seemed no reason to apprehend immediate danger. But those who have most reason to lament his loss, have also most reason to be thankful that he was spared a long illness of anguish and suspense, by so sudden and easy a dismissal.

"To the world at large Bernard Barton was known as the author of much pleasing, amiable, and pious poetry—animated by feeling and fancy—delighting in homely subjects so generally pleasing to English people. He sang of what he loved: the domestic virtues in man, and the quiet pastoral scenes of nature—and especially of his own county—its woods, and fields, and lanes, and homesteads, and the old sea that washed its shores; and the nearer to his own home the better he loved it. There was a true and pure vein of pastoral feeling in him. Thousands have read his books with innocent pleasure: none will ever take them up and be the worse for doing so. The first of these volumes was published in 1811.

"To those of his own neighbourhood he was known as a most amiable, genial, charitable man —of pure, unaffected, unpretending piety—the good neighbour—the cheerful companion—the welcome guest—the hospitable host—tolerant of all men, sincerely attached to many. Few, high or low, but were glad to see him at his customary place in the bank: to exchange some words of kindly greeting with him—few but were glad to have him at their own homes; and there he was the same man, and had the same manners, to all: always equally frank, genial, and communicative, without distinction of rank. He had all George Fox's 'better part,' thorough independence of rank, titles, wealth, and all the distinctions of haberdashery, without making any needless display of such independence. He could dine with Sir Robert Peel one day, and the next sup off bread and cheese with equal relish at a farm-house: and relate with equal enjoyment at the one place what he had seen and heard at the other.

"He was indeed as free from vanity as any man, in spite of the attention which his books drew towards him. If he liked to write, and recite, and print his own occasional verses, it was simply that he himself was interested in them at the time—interested in the subject—in the composition, and amused with the very printing; but he was equally amused with anything his friends had said or written—repeating it everywhere with almost disproportionate relish. And this surely is not a usual mark of vanity.

Indeed, had he had more vanity, he would have written much less, instead of so much: would have altered, and polished, and condensed. Whereas it was all first impulse with him: he never would correct his own verses, though he was perfectly ready to let his friends alter what they chose in them, nay, asked them to do so, so long as he was not called on to assist.

"It was the same with his correspondence, which was one great amusement of his later years. He wrote off as he thought and felt, never pausing to turn a sentence, or to point one; and he was quite content to receive an equally careless reply, so long as it came. He was content with a poem so long as it was good in the main, without minding those smaller beauties which go to make up perfection—content with a letter that told of health and good will, with very little other news—and content with a friend who had the average virtues and accomplishments of men, without being that faultless monster which the world ne'er saw, but so many are half their lives looking for.

"It was the same with his conversation. He never dressed himself for it, whatever company he was going into. He would quote his favourite poems in a farm-house, and tell his humorous Suffolk stories in the genteelest drawing-room—what came into his head at the impulse of the moment came from his tongue: a thing not in general commendable, but wholly pleasant and harmless in one so innocent, so kind, and so agreeable as himself.

"He was excellent company in all companies;

but in none more than in homely parties, in or out of doors, over the winter's fire in the farmhouse or under the tree in summer. He had a cheery word for all : a challenge to good fellowship with the old—a jest with the young— enjoying all, and making all enjoyable and joyous. Many hereabout will long look to that place in their rooms where this good, amiable, and pleasant man used to sit, and radiate good humour around him. Nor can the present writer forget the last out-of-door party he enjoyed with this amiable man : it was in last June, down his favourite Deben to the sea. Though far from well, when once on board he would be cheerful ; was as lively and hearty as any at the little inn at which we disembarked to regale ourselves ; and had a word of cheery salute for every boat or vessel that passed or met us as we drifted home again with a dying breeze at close of evening.

"He was not learned in languages, or in any science of any kind. Even the loftier poetry of our own country he did not much affect. He loved the masters of the homely, the pathetic, and humorous—Crabbe, Cowper, and Goldsmith—for it may surprise many readers of his poems that he had as great a relish for humour —good humoured humour—as any man. And few of his friends will forget him as he used to sit at table, his snuff-box in hand, and a glass of genial wine before him, as he repeated some humorous passage from one of his favourites, glancing his fine brown eyes around the company as he recited. Among prose works, his great favourite was Sir Walter Scott; him he was never tired of reading. He would not allow that one novel was bad, and the best were to him the best of all books. For the last four winters, the present writer has gone through several of these masterpieces with him — generally one night in the week was so employed —Saturday night, which left him free to the prospect of the Sunday's relaxation. Then was the volume taken down impatiently from the shelf, almost before tea was over; and at last, when all was ready, candles snuffed and fire stirred, he would read out, or listen to, those fine stories, one after another, anticipating with a smile, or a glance, the pathetic or humorous turns that *were* coming—enjoying all as much the twentieth time of reading as he had done at the first—till supper coming in closed the book, and recalled him to his genial hospitality, which knew no limit. It was only on Friday last we finished the *Heart of Midlothian*, which he enjoyed, however ill at ease: on Sunday he wanted to know when we should 'begin another novel,' and on Monday night, after a little mortal agony (to use the words of one who loved him best, and by him was best beloved, of all the world) 'that warm heart was still for ever.'

" It would not be fitting to record in a public paper the domestic virtues of a private man. But Bernard Barton was a public man; and the public is pleased, or should be pleased, to know that a writer really *is* as amiable as his books pretend. No common case: especially in the poetic line : where the very sensibilities that constitute the poetic feeling are most apt to revolt

Photo. Welton, Woodbridge.

FITZGERALD'S LODGINGS, MARKET PLACE, WOODBRIDGE.

at the little rubs and discrepancies of common life.

"Scarce a year has elapsed since the death of one of his oldest and dearest friends. Major Moore, whose praise he justly celebrated in verse. Major Moore was also as well known to the public by his books, as much beloved by a large circle of friends. These two men were, perhaps, of equal abilities, though of a different kind: their virtues equal and the same. Long does the memory of such men haunt the places of their mortal abode; stirring within us, perhaps, at the close of many a day, as the sun sets over the scenes with which they were so long associated. It is surely not improper to endeavour to record something to the honour of such men in their own neighbourhoods. Nay, should we not, if we could, make their histories as public as possible? For surely none could honour them without loving them, and, perhaps, unconsciously striving to follow in their footsteps."

In this brief "Memoir" there is much that is characteristic; there are touches that we should recognise as FitzGerald's, if we did not know who had written it. "He could dine with Sir Robert Peel one day, and the next sup off bread and cheese with equal relish at a farm-house, and relate with equal enjoyment at the one place what he had seen and heard at the other" is characteristic of FitzGerald.

To the same journal FitzGerald sent a short report of the funeral on Saturday, March 3rd, 1849, and added three verses of poetry, which are only mediocre, though the last stanza has some merit in it.

The report and verses are as follows:

"FUNERAL OF BERNARD BARTON.—On Monday, February 26th, the mortal remains of Bernard Barton were committed to the earth. A long train of members of the Society to which he belonged, and of old friends and fellow-townsmen, waited to follow him from the door from which he had so often been seen to issue alive and welcome to all eyes. Thus attended, the coffin was borne up the street to the cemetery of the Friends' Meeting-House; and there, surrounded by the grave and decent Brotherhood, and amid the affecting silence of their ceremonial, broken but once by the warning voice of one reverend leader, was lowered down into its final resting-place."

> "Lay him gently in the ground,
>   The good, the genial, and the wise;
>   While spring blows forward in the skies
> To breathe new verdure o'er the mound
>   Where the kindly poet lies.
>
> "Gently lay him in his place,
>   While the still brethren round him stand;
> The soul indeed is far away
> But we would reverence the clay
> In which so long she made a stay,
>   Beaming through the friendly face,
> And holding forth the honest hand—
>
> "Thou, that didst so often twine
>   For other urns the funeral song,
>   One who has known and loved thee long

> Would, ere he mingles with the throng,
> Just hang this little wreath on thine.
>
> "Farewell, thou spirit kind and true;
> Old Friend, for evermore Adieu!"

FitzGerald himself thought very little of these verses, as in a letter written to his friend Cowell in February, 1849, he remarks that he thinks very little of his verses, never having written twenty good ones in his life.

Finding that Barton had left his daughter almost unprovided for, FitzGerald decided to edit and publish, by subscription, a selection of his poems and letters, which with great care and much labour, he did.

FitzGerald's *Euphranor* was published in 1851. He did not think it a particularly good work, referring to it as "a pretty specimen of a chiselled cherry-stone," and he altered it considerably at a later date.

The affairs of FitzGerald's father were now in a desperate muddle. He had been investing all his money in trying to raise coal from his Manchester estate.

Jovial old Squire Jenny had also put £50,000 into the concern, and when the inevitable crash came he lost all.

One morning Squire Jenny drove madly up to the house of Mr. Arthur Biddell, and rushing wildly into the house cried, "Biddell, I want your advice, I'm in a devil of a mess! I'm ruined!"

And it was so, the relentless Manchester vortex had swallowed all and given nothing. The blow undoubtedly led to the death of both, for in a few months Squire Jenny and Mr. FitzGerald, Senr., were in their graves.

During this year, 1851, FitzGerald invited his friend Fanny Kemble to be his guest, and to entertain the good folk of Woodbridge with a reading. He was exceedingly anxious that the "Reading" should be a big success and that the room should be full, the place taken for the occasion being the Lecture Hall close to St. John's Church. FitzGerald personally canvassed his friends, and impressed upon them the importance of being present.

The room was crowded, and when Mrs. Kemble entered FitzGerald rose and bowed to her, and his example was followed by everyone in the room, which much amused Mrs. Kemble.

FitzGerald mounted the platform and introduced his celebrated guest in a few graceful words. Her readings were listened to with intense delight, and her singing of "Oh dear! what can the matter be?" is spoken of in Woodbridge to this day.

Early the next year, whilst at Prees, near to Shrewsbury, on a visit to Archdeacon Allen, FitzGerald was acquainted with the news of his father's death, and at once hurried home. The poor man had never recovered from the colliery crash and his last words were, "That engine works well "—a reference to one of the colliery steam engines. He was buried in the family mausoleum at Boulge.

In 1850 *Polonius* was published, its full title being : *Polonius, A Collection of Wise Saws and Modern Instances*, and it consists, as its title suggests, of a collection of epigrams, most of them from Carlyle, and others from Bacon, Newman, Johnson, etc.

In the following year FitzGerald, who had persevered with his Spanish, published a translation of six of Calderon's plays, named respectively, " The Painter of his own Dishonour," " Keep your own Secret," " Gil Perez," " Three Judgments at a Blow," " The Mayor of Zalamea," and " Beware of Smooth Water."

In July, 1853, FitzGerald goes to what he calls a "great treat," the Ipswich Assizes, where he hopes old Parke (Baron Parke) will have the gout—" he bears it so christianly."

Now FitzGerald's brother John, who has inherited the estates, takes up his residence at Boulge Hall, a sufficient reason for Edward to move from his cottage at the Park Gates, for the brothers were only friends when apart.

CHAPTER IV.

LIFE FROM 1854 TO 1874.

HAVING decided to move from the cottage at Boulge and from the close proximity of his brother, FitzGerald looked about for a lodging. He could not decide immediately upon a suitable place to make his home. He packed up his effects and sent them to Farlingay Hall, a farmhouse in the occupation of Mr. Job Smith, where he was received as a temporary lodger.

Mr. Job Smith had previously lived at the Hall Farm, but this was burned to the ground, and Boulge Hall being empty, Mr. Smith came to reside there. He was the father of Alfred Smith, who, during the latter days of FitzGerald's residence at the Cottage, had acted as his reader, on account of a partial failure of his (FitzGerald's) eyesight.

Mr. Job Smith moved from Boulge Hall shortly before John FitzGerald took up his residence there, and moved into Farlingay Hall, about half-a-mile out of Woodbridge.

Hither then went Edward FitzGerald, and Farlingay remained his headquarters for the next seven years. During these years he wandered much, staying with the Crabbes at Bredfield for months at a time, spending much time with the Cowells at Oxford, and in visits to London and other haunts of his early days.

Of his new lodging he writes to Carlyle under date February 14th, 1854, and tells of a room where he believes even the fastidious Carlyle would sleep comfortably in. He describes his host as taciturn, cautious, honest and active, and says that his host's son could carry him on his shoulders to Ipswich.

In the spring of the same year FitzGerald spent five weeks in Oxford with the Cowells, where he studied Persian, to which Cowell had attracted his attention, in the previous year. In March, owing to the declaration of war by England and France against Russia, Brown had to leave Bedford, being a First-Lieutenant in the Bedfordshire Regular Militia, which regiment had to do Garrison duty at Galway.

Back again in Suffolk FitzGerald buys a sailing boat, in which he sails much on his beloved Deben.

Early in the next year (January, 1855) Mrs. FitzGerald, Edward's mother, died and was buried at Boulge, where in the church may be seen a large and handsome monumental tablet to her memory. Beside it is a smaller and less significant one to her husband, illustrating, as Miss Margaret White says in *The Idler* of July, 1900, " the proportion they bore to each other in life."

In the summer of the following year Carlyle,

who had been overworking himself on his *Frederick*, felt the need of a change and decided to fulfil a promise made to FitzGerald, to stay a while with him. Though honoured by the proposed visit and delighted at the prospect of seeing his friend, FitzGerald looks forward to the visit with a certain amount of apprehension —he knew his Carlyle. He asks Mrs. Carlyle what her husband is to eat, drink and avoid, and assures Carlyle that he will have perfect freedom, etc., etc. Carlyle replies : " It will be pleasant to see your face at the end of my shrieking, mad, (and to me quite horrible) rail operations. . . . I hope to get to Farlingay not long after four o'clock, and have a quiet mutton chop in due time, and have a ditto pipe or pipes : nay, I could even have a bathe if there was any sea water left in the evening."

FitzGerald met him at Ipswich and drove him to Farlingay. The visit was a complete success. The two great men had walks through the delightful woods and lanes of the district, drives to historic Dunwich, and the once-great Framlingham. A visit to Aldeburgh delighted Carlyle; he described the fishing hamlet as " a beautiful, quasi-deserted little sea town . . . Nothing can excel the sea—a mile of fine, shingly beach, with patches of smooth sand every here and there; clear water shelving rapidly, deep at all hours, beach solitary beyond wont, whole town rather solitary."

FitzGerald shews at his best as the kind, courteous host. He took an exultant pride in displaying the beauties of his native county to his august guest: he "discharged the sacred rites with a kind of Irish zeal and piety."

Carlyle returned to London by steamer, refusing to be suffocated in a railway carriage, "like a great codfish in a hamper." A month later he wrote to FitzGerald: "On the whole I say, when you get your little Suffolk cottage, you must have in it a 'chamber in the wall' for me, *plus* a pony that can trot, and a cow that gives good milk; with these outfits we shall make a pretty rustication now and then, not wholly Latrappish, but only *half*, on much easier terms than here; and I for one shall be right willing to come and try it, I for one party. . . After the beginning of next week, I am at Chelsea, and (I dare say) there is a fire in the evenings now to welcome you there. Show face in some way or other. And so adieu, for my hour of riding is at hand."

Another cloud overspread the horizon. His much-loved Cowell accepted a Professorship of History at Calcutta, and FitzGerald mourned for him as dead. Not daring to bid Cowell and his wife farewell, he writes to tell them that it is best that he should not see them again to say a good-bye that would cost him so much, and that he hoped to keep up something of a correspondence with them and he hoped they would do the same.

In another letter to Cowell he tells him that he has seen in an Ipswich paper that he is appointed duly to the post, and says that he must have their portraits and that he cannot again look at him or his wife.

When we realise what passions FitzGerald's friendships were, we know that those words, " I can't look at you and her again," were wrung from a breaking heart. Gone the Bramford days! Gone the Oxford days! Gone his best-loved friends!

In 1856 came the catastrophe of FitzGerald's life, his one great mistake—the marriage with Lucy Barton. The real facts of this ill-starred alliance are not known, or rather the events that led up to it. That Edward FitzGerald had contemplated marriage with Lucy Barton for years, seems evident. He may have construed his promise to his dead friend, the father of Lucy, to look after his child, as a kind of half-promise of marriage.

W. K. Brown, who probably knew FitzGerald and his temperament better than anyone, and had no small knowledge of Lucy Barton, did everything in his power to prevent the union; he pointed out that FitzGerald was veering towards a precipice, and that unhappiness would come to both through the marriage! (Alas! how true!) FitzGerald said that he had seriously considered the matter and that he had pledged his word to take care of Miss Barton. He seemed to think that he was pledged to Miss Barton, though if any actual engagement had occurred it is impossible to tell. That he was not in love is apparent. There was no courting. FitzGerald was forty-seven and Miss Barton forty-nine. He probably looked forward to simply a quiet settling down after his many wanderings—he looked forward to having a home—nothing more.

The marriage ceremony took place on November 4th, 1856, at All Saints' Church, Chichester, where some friends of Miss Barton were living at the time.

Immediately after the wedding they went to Brighton for a few days, and then to Great Portland Street, London. The wife that he had married was careful, fussy even, and prim, particularly careful over matters of attire, and in every respect the antithesis of FitzGerald; so right at the start of their married life misunderstandings arose, and during the first eleven weeks of their wedded life Mrs. FitzGerald stayed away from her husband with friends for five consecutive weeks. For two months they lived unhappily together in apartments in Regent's Park, and then FitzGerald saw that separation must come. In a pathetic letter to his friend Professor Cowell, he asks him to address his letters to Bredfield Rectory, as, in his unsettled state, he could fix no place to live or die in.

He wrote a letter to George Crabbe from London—full of pathos, a letter from a man just waking to a sense of his misery. He wishes his friend a good new year and points out that he is in London alone, his wife having gone to Geldestone and he is staying in London to arrange business matters.

He is in a total quandary about a place of abode. His wife suggests Norwich, but accommodation could not be found there, so he thinks they may go to Lowestoft for a time. He wants his wife to learn housekeeping as he thinks her hand is out of practice. He talks of joining his wife at Geldestone in a few days to try to arrange matters. At London he says he has scarcely seen anyone, and remarks what a waste of life it is, if ever his life could be worth living, and he adds pitifully that he is rather weary of it.

There are people living at Woodbridge to-day who have distinct recollections of Mrs. Fitz-Gerald, and they speak of her as a highly cultured, well-educated woman, fitted to move in the highest society, and of some literary ability. When she married FitzGerald, a man of some means, perhaps it was but natural that she should desire to go into society and herself to entertain. Such a life would be particularly distasteful to a man of FitzGerald's Bohemian temperament. FitzGerald, careless, unconventional, disorderly in dress, with a horror of having to "dress" for dinner, possibly a man who should never have married at all, or if he did, should have chosen a woman of great tact and endless resource, which Mrs. FitzGerald certainly was *not*.

These were dark days for FitzGerald, everything seemed tinged with his sadness, the past, the hallowed past, reposed behind him like a dream of Paradise. His present sorrows only revived the colours of bygone pictures. By one turn of fate's wheel all was changed; well might he say, when wistfully looking back over his paradise lost, "I believe there are new channels fretted in my cheeks with many unmanly tears since then."

FitzGerald and his wife tried life in the country for a short time, living at Gorleston, near Yarmouth, but things went on no better, and, not able to endure it any longer, FitzGerald decided on a separation and they parted. Not only for his own sake—FitzGerald was never selfish—but for his wife's, he saw that this was the only course that would be best for her and make life endurable for himself.

During the brief period that FitzGerald and his wife lived together he consoled himself with his Persian studies, especially with the works of the Persian poet Attar. Obtaining a manuscript of the *Mautik-ut-Tair*, or Bird Parliament, he set to work translating it into English.

He now took up the threads of his life

where he had dropped them six months before. For a time he took up his abode at Bredfield Rectory and Farlingay Hall. Much talk followed his return to Woodbridge without his wife, and one can well understand his reasons for calling his yacht the "Scandal." He determined to live down the talk and continued to reside in the neighbourhood of Woodbridge. His friends remained true, being convinced that he made the great mistake of his life from a noble and generous impulse.

In 1857, George Crabbe, who had been ailing for some time, died, a great loss, not only to FitzGerald, but to the whole neighbourhood, for the Vicar of Bredfield was greatly beloved by rich and poor alike.

Scarcely was the funeral, which FitzGerald attended, over, when another great blow almost overwhelmed him. His beloved friend and hero, W. Kenworthy Browne, met with an accident whilst out riding, from the effects of which he died. He was out hunting at Great Barford near Bedford, when his horse reared and fell over upon him, and he was taken home to Goldington, dying. He lingered, however, for many weeks in great agony. Well-nigh broken-hearted, FitzGerald hurried to Goldington and stayed with his friend to the end; he writes to Mr. Aldis Wright, describing his visit and how he stood by the bedside, and dwelling upon the virtues of his lost friend.

It was now (1859) that the first edition of "The Rubáiyát of Omar Khayyám" was published. FitzGerald printed 250 copies, but, financially, it was a failure. It was on sale at one shilling and not as stated by both Mr. John Glyde and Prof. E. D. Ross, at five shillings. An advertisement in *The Athenæum* of April 9th, 1859, reads, "*Just published, price 1/-, 'Rubáiyát of Omar Khayyám,' the Astronomer-Poet of Persia, translated into English Verse. B. Quaritch, London, Castle Street, Leicester Square.*"

In 1860 FitzGerald moved into new lodgings, over a gun-maker's shop in the Market Place, Woodbridge. (The house is now occupied by a plumber named Nunn, and let into the wall is a stone tablet bearing the initials E. F. G. and the dates 1860-1873.) Here he brought his books and his pictures and settled down to his lonely life and his writing. The latter he had no occasion to do for a living, for at his mother's death he was left an income of a thousand pounds a year. His host or landlord at Farlingay Hall, Mr. Job Smith, had died, and his son, FitzGerald's reader, settled on the other side of the Deben at Sutton.

During all the years that he lived at the Market Place (thirteen) FitzGerald spent a great deal of his time on the water. His letters of this period are full of references to his yacht, the Deben, the sea, sailors and fisherfolk. His yacht, "The Scandal," named after the staple of

Woodbridge, was a familiar sight on the river and at the sea-ports on the Suffolk and Norfolk coast. He engaged as his captain a man named Thomas Newton, a smart sailor, who spoke through his nose and had a peculiar habit of holding his head awry, as FitzGerald said "like a magpie looking in a quart pot." He was a jovial fellow, however, and always happy. FitzGerald once said of him: "He is always smiling, yet the wretched fellow is the father of twins." This skipper gave a different account of the origin of the name of the yacht. In a letter to the *East Anglian Daily Times* in July, 1889, Mr. Spalding, a friend of FitzGerald's, says: "I was standing with him (the Captain) on the Lowestoft Fish Market, close to which the little 'Scandal' was moored, after an early dive from her deck, when Tom was addressed by one of two ladies: 'Pray, my man, can you tell me who owns that very pretty yacht?' 'Mr. Edward FitzGerald, of Woodbridge, ma'am,' said Tom, touching his cap. 'And can you tell us her name?' 'The "Scandal," ma'am.' 'Dear me! how came he to select such a very peculiar name?' 'Well, ma'am, the fact is, all the other names were taken up, so that we were forced to have either that or none.' The ladies at once moved on."

Boating was now and hereafter the chief amusement of FitzGerald's life, he was happiest going in his little boat round the coast, taking as refreshment bottled porter and bread and cheese.

In 1863, Mrs. Kerrich, FitzGerald's best-loved sister, died. FitzGerald was too heart-broken to attend the funeral. He spoke of her as one sacrificing everything for her children, never thinking of herself, and said that he would not go to the funeral, where there would be plenty of mourners.

In the same year, the friend and companion of his youth, the great Thackeray, died, and FitzGerald feels more lonely than ever, but seeks consolation on sea and river.

In April, 1864, he went on a visit to Miss Caroline Crabbe, in Wiltshire, and spent many happy days with, what many would have us think, the sweetheart of his youth. Returning to Woodbridge he bought from a friend, Major Pytches, of Melton, a farm-house in the north-east of Woodbridge. It was called "Grange Farm," but at the request of Miss Anna Biddell, FitzGerald altered the name to "Little Grange." At the head of many of his letters appear a pointing hand and " Little Grange " and under it in brackets ("by Anna Biddell's order-mark!") or (" Anna ordered this change of name ").

Though he bought himself a house, and a very charming one too, FitzGerald continued to live, partly at his lodgings on Market Hill and partly on his schooner yacht, the "Scandal."

After an absence of eight years in India his

beloved friends, the Cowells, returned to England, but the event only gave FitzGerald "a sad sort of pleasure, dashed with the memory of other days."

Now comes the time when FitzGerald made that strange, in many ways inexplicable, friendship with the stalwart fisherman, Joseph Fletcher, "Posh," a man who apparently had little to recommend him save his size and his "Saxon type" and perhaps his almost stupid simplicity. And yet FitzGerald idolised him, almost worshipped him, had his portrait painted to hang with Thackeray's and Tennyson's, his "three great friends, but 'Posh' is the greatest." Even his faults were virtues to FitzGerald. After a drunken bout on the part of his idol, FitzGerald writes to Spalding, making every excuse for his friend's failing, declaring that he was ashamed to play the judge on one who was far above him, and saying that his faults were better than many virtues. Later on FitzGerald built a herring-lugger for "Posh," entering into a kind of partnership, from which it is feared he saw but little profit and much loss. "Posh" seems to have brought back some of the former joy into the life of FitzGerald: his letters are full of him, he entertains him like a lord at his rooms and in hotels, takes him to theatres and indeed seems as though he cannot do enough for him.

It was whilst in the company of Fletcher that

FitzGerald once—the only time after the separation—saw his wife. Mrs. FitzGerald occasionally came to Woodbridge, where of course she had many friends. On these visits she would stay with Dr. Jones, and FitzGerald always went away from the town during these visits, doubtless to avoid a meeting that would prove painful to both.

One day FitzGerald and " Posh " were walking down the Woodbridge Thoroughfare when he saw a female figure approaching them. " Posh ! " he whispered, " it's my wife ! " Mrs. FitzGerald held out her hand, but it was not taken by her husband : " Come along Posh ! " he exclaimed, and walked rapidly away.

Meanwhile FitzGerald had written much. In 1860 he contributed a series of articles signed " F." to the *East Anglian Daily Times*, and in the same and following year came the *Parathina* contributions, twelve in number, to *Notes and Queries*. A reprint of the first edition of " Omar " was also published in 1862, and two more of the translations of Calderon's plays, *The Mighty Magician* and *Such Stuff as Dreams are Made of*, came in 1865. The same year also saw the publication of the first edition of *Agamemnon*.

FitzGerald's house, Little Grange, was undergoing considerable alterations at the hands of a Mr. Dove, a Woodbridge builder, more, it appears, to find work for some unemployed men at Woodbridge than to prepare it for residence. FitzGerald, was, or appeared to be, very hard to please; after certain alterations had been completed he would suddenly discover that he did not like it and down it would come. This occurred several times, and though it sorely tried the patience of Mr. Dove, it prolonged the work for men who would not otherwise have been employed.

Meanwhile FitzGerald's brother John had become more eccentric than ever. He was everlastingly preaching at all the village chapels within a twenty mile radius of Boulge, or conducting anti-Romanist crusades. His sermons were of a tremendous length, and during the delivery of them he would indulge in weird contortions and gesticulations, moving the candlesticks from side to side, even waving them aloft, with a consequent baptism of grease. He would, before preaching, give his watch to one person, his handkerchief to another, and keys and purse to whoever would take them. He was as mad at his hall at Boulge as he was in the pulpit. He had a clock in every room and yet when he required to know the time would ring for his valet and ask him.

Edward FitzGerald spent more time than ever on the water, and every year dreaded more and more the winter, which would largely confine him to his Market Hill lodgings. He sailed to Lowestoft, Yarmouth, Aldeburgh, up the Orwell to Ipswich, and occasionally across to Holland.

He continued to cheerfully lose money over his partnership in the fishing lugger he had built for " Posh," and to entertain his " hero " and his " hero's " wife and even his " hero's " chums.

A pathetic little story is told of a visit of "Posh" and FitzGerald to Yarmouth. Passing through Gorleston, FitzGerald said to " Posh," " I want you to turn down here, I want to go and see the house where I lived with my wife." Reaching the spot he said: " Stop! Ah! Ah! 'Posh,' had you but come to me at Lowestoft *then!* If I had only known you at that time, when I used to wander on those hills—unhappy! "—pointing to the Gorleston uplands—" Her ways were not my ways, and we parted. Drive on, there's a good fellow! "

In 1867 FitzGerald became acquainted with Mr. W. Aldis Wright, the bursar of Trinity College, Cambridge, an acquaintance which soon ripened into a warm friendship. To Mr. Aldis Wright was entrusted the editing of FitzGerald's works. With great patience he devoted himself to the difficult task of collecting and editing FitzGerald's letters and to him the world owes no small amount of gratitude for arranging and publishing these masterpieces of English—second, perhaps, to none in the language.

FitzGerald was now over 60 years of age and his old affection of the eyes, which he had first experienced in the Boulge Cottage and suffered from more or less ever since, now got worse. In consequence, he sold his yacht, the "Scandal," for £200 as he could no longer see to read in the cabin. He had now to employ another boy reader, whom he named the "Blunderer." This lad was the son of a Woodbridge cabinet maker named Hayward, and is still alive and residing in Church Street, Woodbridge. I had a long conversation with this boy reader—now, of course, a man—and he related to me the whole story of his connection with Edward FitzGerald and some new anecdotes which are told in the chapter headed "Character—Reminiscences."

He was reader to FitzGerald on and off for five years. He says that FitzGerald was greatly amused at his reading of the Titchborne Trial—but whether the amusement was derived from the subject matter or from the ludicrous mistakes of the reader is not known—probably the latter. FitzGerald, he told me, would sit back in his chair and ha! ha! ha! until he, the reader, was quite disconcerted. With him FitzGerald often played cards, playing a game with a French name which he could not now remember. FitzGerald would express considerable satisfaction when he, the reader, won, but when his constant winning became monotonous, the reading would be resumed. FitzGerald never would pay him personally for his services but settled up periodically with his father.

He preferred him to any other boy he had, probably on account of the amusement his blunders provoked, "'ironic' laughter from the extreme left," became "ironclad" laughter; there were "face-smiles of letters," "proposition" became a "proposed position," and in the stock market "Consolations closed at 91."

At this time FitzGerald made frequent visits to the once famous, but now lost, town of Dunwich. FitzGerald came to love the ancient place and spent much time there. Here it was that he met Charles Keene of *Punch*, who became his firm friend, and Keene frequently stayed at Little Grange after FitzGerald settled there.

Following in FitzGerald's footsteps I paid a visit to Dunwich.

Centuries ago Dunwich was the most important town in East Anglia, boasting a Royal Mint, a Palace and, we are told, over fifty churches. It has been swallowed by the sea. The town is gone, and far out, fathoms down beneath the blue waters of the German ocean, are its remains, covered by the sand.

I stood in the ruins of its one remaining church, that of All Saints, standing on the very edge of the cliffs, only waiting its turn to fall into the sea and mingle its remains with those of the ancient town. I climbed down the cliff and found myself in the ancient churchyard, at my elbow was a stone coffin, broken in halves and protruding from the cliff, at my feet was a heap of human bones, which centuries before had been buried here with their mortal coverings. Down on the beach was a heap of masonry, a part of the East end of the church lately fallen, and soon, very soon, the rest of the church must go the same way.

FitzGerald's friend Bernard Barton wrote a poem of considerable merit on Dunwich and it was in the company of the poet that FitzGerald first visited the little hamlet, all that remains of a once mighty town.

In December, 1873, FitzGerald's landlord, Mr. Berry, married again and this meant that FitzGerald must leave his Market Hill lodgings, to which he had become much attached. The story of how Mr. Berry gave FitzGerald notice to quit has been told more than once, but it may be new to some. FitzGerald, who was fond of chatting with Berry, did not relish the introduction of the new element, and told him so, adding that, "old Berry would now have to be called 'Old Gooseberry!'" This was repeated to the widow; and resulted in Berry giving him notice to quit. Berry did not like the task of breaking with his old friend and lodger, and came cautiously upstairs to announce the decision. His helpmeet, fearing that his courage might give way, remained at the bottom of the stairs, calling out: "Be firm, Berry! Remind him of what he called you." Berry accordingly entered the room trembling and with many apologies told FitzGerald that he must go, and fearing to meet his new spouse with but half his message delivered he added, "and I have been told, sir, that you have called me 'Old Gooseberry.'"

Instead of going immediately to his own house, which had long been furnished and used by his friends and relatives, he hired a room next door to his old lodgings and stayed there a short time, but soon moved into his last "lodging"—the charming Little Grange.

CHAPTER V.

LIFE, 1874, TO DEATH, 1883.

AT Little Grange, FitzGerald occupied but one room, a large apartment in the new part of the house which he himself had added. The entrance-hall contained an organ, upon which FitzGerald delighted to play. He always played from memory, all the old songs; and his heart was wrung as he played them: back came crowding the memories of days long dead—bringing with them the ghosts of his old loves. Keene sketched his *body* at this organ, but he could not sketch his *soul*, nor picture that great heart, breaking with a poignant remembrance.

French windows in the study opened upon a long, delightful walk with a high elm hedge on one side. This FitzGerald called his Quarter-deck and would saunter here sometimes alone, but always with his memories. He loved his garden, with its old-world flowers and its subtle perfumes and his greenhouse containing an oleander, of which he says: " Don't you love the oleander? so clean in its leaves and stem, so beautiful in its flower. I rather worship mine." The garden at Little Grange was, during FitzGerald's time, a galaxy of colour—FitzGerald loved colours, he had a veneration, almost an adoration for all things bright and beautiful, the radiant morn, the crimson of the sunset sky. Turnerlike pictures and gorgeous flowers were a source of endless delight to him; roses and nasturtiums were his favourite flowers and these were found in abundance in his garden.

These may appear but trifling things to mention, but they are the little characteristics which were very noticeable in the life of FitzGerald. I asked a man, a life-long friend of his, what were the outstanding features in the character of the poet, and he replied, " His love of using capital letters and his passion for gay colours." To prove that this impression was correct, one has only to remember his garden and look at his letters. He often deplored the lack of colour in grey England. " The Englishman," he said, " hates rich colours, and especially where they are most needed to warm and light up his cold, colourless skies and seas."

When he was at Little Grange, FitzGerald wrote many of his most beautiful letters and those to Fanny Kemble are among his very best. She was always his great friend, and the letters that he wrote to her are very beautiful, tender, fanciful, gracefully critical, sometimes witty and at all times affectionate. They extended in an almost unbroken series from 1871 to the time of his death in 1883. These letters were published in 1885. In the *Atlantic Monthly*, Mrs. Kemble contributed some Fitz-Gerald sketches, in which she lavishly praises her old friend, too lavishly indeed for Fitz-Gerald, for in his copy he pasted strips of paper over the more extravagant eulogies.

"A poet, a painter," she grandiloquently exclaims, "a musician, an admirable scholar and writer, if he had not shunned notoriety as sedulously as most people seek it, he would have achieved a foremost place among the eminent men of the day."

FitzGerald had for his servants—though he treated them more like friends—one, John Howe, and Howe's wife Mary Anne. John Howe was a delightfully simple soul, who " spelt his name H-o-w as a rule, but on important occasions, such as weddings, funerals or christenings, added an ' e,' a custom still preserved in the family; and spoke with a nasal twang in the Suffolk vernacular, always addressing his master as Mr. Fitz-Jarel." He was as great a source of amusement to FitzGerald as his second reader had been, and his quaint way of talking, as well as his droll ideas, were the cause of considerable mirth to FitzGerald and his friends. He was called by his master, " My old Hermes," " The King of Clubs "—his face somewhat resembling the club as seen on playing cards—" Old Puddledog," because of his many blunders. His wife, Mrs. Howe, was a favourite with FitzGerald and she always wore, by his request, a red dress and a red cloak, more pleasing to FitzGerald than a "hundred coats-of-arms." To her he gave the name of "The Fairy Godmother," and to both her husband and herself he always showed much kindness, even devotion.

In 1874, FitzGerald, who now travelled less frequently than formerly, paid a long contemplated visit to Scotland to see some of the haunts of Sir Walter Scott, whose works he was never tired of reading and praising. He stayed in Scotland but a very short time; he heard Suffolk calling, and after three days hurried back to Woodbridge.

FitzGerald's brother Peter died at Bournemouth in February, 1875. Between Edward and Peter FitzGerald there was always considerable love. Peter often voyaged with his brother in the "Scandal" and his last words were, "Edward! Edward! Edward!"

In September, 1876, Alfred Tennyson, accompanied by his son Hallam, paid FitzGerald a visit at Woodbridge. Thinking that his house was not sufficiently comfortable for his guests, he engaged rooms for them at the Bull Inn, close to his old lodging. The Bull Inn was kept by a man who was a friend of FitzGerald's, named John Grout. Talking with FitzGerald after the departure of the Tennysons, he asked who the visitors were. "Tennyson, the Poet Laureate; and you should consider your house honoured by his presence," answered FitzGerald. "Dissày" (Suffolk for "daresay,"), answered Grout. "Anyhow, he didn't fare to know much about hosses, when I showed him over my stables."

On alighting at Woodbridge station Tennyson enquired where "Mr. Edward FitzGerald" lived, and was directed to a house in Seckforde Street. Tennyson and his son made their way to the spot indicated and knocked at the door of the house. It was opened by a policeman. "Does Mr. Edward FitzGerald live here?" asked Tennyson. "Yes" answered the policeman, "that's my name." Tennyson did not recognise in the form before him, his old friend, and thinking that during the twenty years that had elapsed since he had last seen FitzGerald, that he might have taken to the law, he made further enquiries and discovered that this was another Mr. Edward FitzGerald, the Superintendent of the County police, who kindly took the visitors to the house of his namesake.

The next day FitzGerald took his guests to Ipswich by steamer and shewed them round the ancient town. Returning to Woodbridge they spent many happy hours in the garden at Little Grange, where Tennyson was much struck with the picture of FitzGerald seated under a tree, with his grey locks gently disturbed by the breezes, and his doves alighting on and feeding out of his hand, and he pictures the scene in the Dedication to his *Tiresias*:—

> "Old Fitz, who from your suburb grange,
>   Where once I tarried for a while,
> Glance at the wheeling Orb of change,
>   And greet it with a kindly smile;
> Whom yet I see as there you sit
>   Beneath your sheltering garden-tree,
> And while your doves about you flit,
>   And plant on shoulder, hand, and knee,
> Or on your head their rosy feet,
>   As if they knew your diet spares
> Whatever moved in that full sheet,
>   Let down to Peter at his prayers;
> Who live on milk and meal and grass."

In the years 1877 and 1879 FitzGerald contributed to the *Ipswich Journal* some short articles on subjects of local interest, signing them "Effigy," a pun on his initials E. F. G. and these are of much interest, especially to East Anglians.

During these years at Little Grange, he was cheered by the occasional visits of Charles Keene, who would march up and down the "Quarter-deck" playing the bagpipes, an accomplishment of which he was inordinately proud, but FitzGerald would only allow him to play them in the house if he "took the drone off." He was a man after FitzGerald's own heart, revelling in untidiness and tobacco smoke, careless in his attire, fond of music and a master with the pencil. There were many delightful little dinner parties, at which Keene, Archdeacon Groome, Herman Biddell and FitzGerald would relate the humorous stories of the day.

One which greatly amused FitzGerald was told by the Archdeacon. A certain churchyard in Suffolk was utilised by the clergyman for another purpose than its ostensible one, namely the growing of potatoes. "Really" said the Archdeacon to the Clergyman, "I don't like to see this!" whereupon the old churchwarden who was standing by exclaimed, "That's what I say, Mr. Archdeacon, you go on a tatering and a tatering, why don't you wheat it?"

When no friends were at Little Grange, FitzGerald would content himself with his books and his flowers. Among his favourite books were the works of Crabbe, Scott. some of Dickens', Macready's *Reminiscences*, *Wesley's Journal*—esteemed very highly and which he many times talked of abridging—*Don Quixote* and the *Decameron*.

In 1876 FitzGerald lost his reader and in his place obtained another, a lad named Fox, son of a Woodbridge bookbinder. This lad he named—he had a nickname for everyone—"The Ghost"—because he would always appear so suddenly and punctually. In connection with Fox, a little incident with a flavour of Omar's philosophy, occurred. FitzGerald lost his spectacles and when "The Ghost" asked if he should help to look for them, FitzGerald replied, "No, I suppose that is the way I shall get to heaven, searching for what I cannot find."

FitzGerald was at Lowestoft again about

LITTLE GRANGE, WOODBRIDGE. *Photo. Welton, Woodbridge.*

FARLINGAY HALL.
(Where Carlyle stayed with FitzGerald.) *Photo. Welton, Woodbridge.*

this time. He occupied his same old room in Marine Terrace, and it was a melancholy pleasure for him to see the yacht which he had built for "Posh," the *Meum and Tuum*—" Mum and Tum" the fishermen called it—come into the harbour, and to see his hero-captain, "Posh," upon whom he still continued to shower a prodigious amount of affection.

During the early days of his life at Little Grange FitzGerald had consulted a doctor about his health, which at this time caused him some anxiety. He was informed that his heart was affected, a piece of news which he hailed with joy. Meeting an acquaintance a few days after the medical examination, he congratulated him upon a similar affection, saying, "I congratulate you; I have heart trouble myself, and am glad of it. I don't want a posse of old women round me when I am dying,"—a wish that was to be ultimately realised.

The year 1879 sees FitzGerald up at London on one of his annual visits. He drops in at the Lyceum to see Irving play "Hamlet," and did not think much of the acting. He stood at the back of the pit and endured two acts, and then with an exclamation of impatience went out. This was doubtless largely due to the mood of the moment; often when irritable he was inclined to be harsh in his criticisms, and at this time his melancholy was increased by the loss, by death, of many friends. He was now seventy, but his mental powers were still vigorous, and this year (1879) he published at his own expense a selection of Crabbe's *Tales of the Hall*. The work has never been widely read and was not a great success. FitzGerald did it mainly to call attention to Crabbe's book, and partly on account of an article that appeared in the *Cornhill* in which the writer calls Crabbe a "Pope in worsted stockings." FitzGerald indignantly exclaimed " Pope in worsted stockings! Why, I could cite whole paragraphs of as fine a texture as Molière; 'incapable of epigram' the Jackanape says; why, I could find fifty of the very best epigrams in five minutes."

Three hundred and fifty copies of FitzGerald's abridgment were printed and many of them distributed among his friends.

Edward FitzGerald's eccentric brother died on May 4th of this year (1879), amidst a great many worries and troubles which came upon him suddenly. Edward FitzGerald comments on the sad event thus, " My poor brother died very suddenly. In fact he had ordered his carriage, intending to take a drive. . . . We were very good friends of very different ways of thinking."

John FitzGerald's second child, Gerald, died a month after his father, and his third child, Maurice, had died eighteen months before; some relatives are still living in California.

Edward now seemed very much alone, his friends fell about him like wheat before the scythe, and a deep melancholy sat upon him, which he tried in vain to throw off. His Dunwich friend, Edwin Edwards, with whom he had spent many of his happiest days, walking among the ruins on the Dunwich Cliff, seeking the unique Dunwich roses, now died in London. At the same time the sister of Mrs. Kemble died. FitzGerald determined, in spite of his inclination to stay more and more at home, to go to London and call upon both Mrs. Edwards and Mrs. Kemble.

He found Mrs. Edwards broken-hearted and inconsolable, and the meeting touched FitzGerald deeply. Mrs. Kemble he found grieved at her loss but less demonstrative than Mrs. Edwards. She and FitzGerald spent many hours together, talking over the tender past and their common friends. Early the next year he paid another visit to Mrs. Kemble.

In June of the same year, he went to Merton on a visit to the Rev. George Crabbe (son of the Vicar of Bredfield and grandson of the poet), and revelled in the glorious country scenery, the yellow clay cottages and red-tiled roofs.

Back again in Woodbridge, the health of FitzGerald gave some anxiety, and the increasing heart trouble gave warning of the approaching end. Now his friend and master, Carlyle, died (February 4th, 1881), and the next month James Spedding was run over and carried dying to St. George's Hospital.

In 1881 he went to see the Cowells at Cambridge, and in 1882 to London to see his friend Donne, who was dying, and again to see Mrs. Kemble.

FitzGerald's declining years were cheered and his youthful memories revived by a renewal of his acquaintance with Mary Lynn, with whom he had played on the sands of Aldeburgh sixty years before. Indeed he now had an irresistible longing to renew the friendships of his early days. Few—very few—of his early friends were left, and he felt anxious to make the most of those that were yet left to him ere they " too into the Dust descend."

In 1882 he again went to stay at Aldeburgh and took apartments at his usual house, " Clarke Cottage," and this time Charles Keene accompanied him and enlivened the time with his beloved bagpipes.

FitzGerald was now an old man, 74 years of age, with eyes which scarcely saw, a hacking cough and weak heart, and he felt himself that his end was near. He made his will and set other matters in order. Among other bequests he left £1,000 to Miss Caroline Crabbe, £500 to Anne Ritchie, daughter of Thackeray, £1,000 to be divided among the daughters of the Rev. William Airy, £1,000 for the daughters of Frederick Tennyson. The bulk of his property he left to the residuary legatees, the children of his sister, Mrs. Kerrich.

At Easter, whilst Mr. Aldis Wright was visiting him, FitzGerald talked of the deaths in the family and remarked that both his mother and brother John died at 75. "None of us get beyond 75," he said.

His much-loved summer—the last he was to see—came, and with it his roses and nasturtiums. Again he walked up and down his "Quarterdeck," again he rejoiced in the glorious colours of the spring and delighted his heart with the perfumes of his garden, and had no immediate warning of the coming shadow—the shadow of the Valley.

On June 13th he wrote the letter mentioned in Chapter I. and the next day set off on a visit to the Crabbes at Merton in Norfolk. Still anxious to revive the memories of the past he travelled by Bury St. Edmunds that he might see his old school—the school where he had made some of those friendships which he himself said were "more like loves."

At Watton Station George Crabbe met him and drove to Merton Rectory, FitzGerald talking cheerfully on the way.

At tea he talked much of Bury and Bury days with George and Miss Caroline Crabbe (who was on a visit to her brother). He was somewhat tired on account of the long journey from Woodbridge and his rambles around Bury, so retired to bed early. As he did not come down next morning, a servant was sent to his room and receiving no response to her knock she entered and found him peacefully lying in bed asleep—and dead. He had gone to his Great Reunion, to join his lost loves—he had solved Omar's riddle.

His body was taken to Little Grange and from thence to Boulge Churchyard, where he was buried in the bosom of his Mother-earth and not in the FitzGerald Mausoleum. It was his wish to be buried "where the birds sing."

> "So bury me by some sweet Garden-side."
> * * * *
> "That ev'n my buried Ashes such a Snare
> Of Perfume shall fling up into the air."

The funeral was attended by many of his surviving friends; and the Poet Laureate, his great friend Alfred Tennyson, sent a wreath.

A granite slab covers the grave, and on it is inscribed, "Edward FitzGerald, born 31st March 1809, died 14th June 1883"; and the text which he himself selected, "It is He that hath made us and not we ourselves."

The Omar Khayyám Club, with several friends and well-known literary men, made a pilgrimage to the grave on October 7th, 1893, and planted thereon a rose tree, which was raised from seed brought from the grave of Omar Khayyám at Naishapur. So, though eight hundred years have passed away since the death of Omar, the rose petals from his grave fall every summer at the head of FitzGerald, whispering to him in that strange Eastern tongue he loved so well.

CHAPTER VI.

Character—Reminiscences.

I HAVE spent many long and delightful hours with the few remaining friends of Edward FitzGerald. I have wandered round his house at Woodbridge—charming Little Grange. I have strolled round Bredfield White House, his birthplace, and have stood in that delightful little Boulge Cottage in company of those who daily met and conversed with him. I know FitzGerald through his friends, I know him through the many Woodbridge folk who might be termed his acquaintances, I know him through those who worked for him on his yacht the "Scandal" or in his house and garden at Woodbridge, or who read to him in his declining years at Little Grange.

It is a land of roses, this FitzGerald country. Roses—roses everywhere—a prodigality of roses, every breeze is laden with their fragrance, the setting sun shines right *through* them, turning

"That yellow cheek of hers to incarnadine."

Surely it was such a rose as this that with the zephyr breaks and floats in a perfumed shower of petals to the ground, that started Omar on his playful sceptical musings eight hundred years ago, and the same rose was blowing and dying when FitzGerald took up the medley of Eastern colours, and by his genius transformed them into the pattern of the matchless Rubáiyát.

Edward FitzGerald had three outstanding characteristics, an intense love for his friends, a love of nature generally and the sea in particular, and a love for the past. He was a man of wonderful simplicity of life and of great kindness of heart, a perfect gentleman, generous of heart and hand, and intensely sympathetic.

Eccentric he certainly was—as were all the FitzGeralds—an eccentricity arising largely from absent-mindedness or pre-occupation. Eccentric only in trivialities, never in principles. It would be quite conceivable that FitzGerald would boil his watch and time it by the egg, or as he often did, spend a pound to save two-and-sixpence, not because he was parsimonious but because saving the half-crown never occurred to him.

An incident in the life of FitzGerald, told me by a man who knew him well, will explain this exactly.

FitzGerald was going to London from Woodbridge to see some of his friends, taking with him his handy-man. When they left Woodbridge the sky was clear—it always is at Woodbridge—but when they arrived at the London station it was raining in torrents. FitzGerald paced rest-

lessly up and down the platform, expressing his
regret at having omitted to bring his umbrella,
and every now and then sent his man out to see
if the rain had ceased. Suddenly FitzGerald
stopped in front of a time-table. His long
artistic fingers followed the dotted lines and
then he referred to his watch.

Presently he turned to his man and said:
"John, go and fetch my umbrella and catch
the . . . train back." And faithful John
went to Woodbridge and back, a distance of
about 160 miles and costing about twice as
much as an umbrella could have been purchased
for just outside the station, whilst FitzGerald
stayed in the waiting-room.

To anyone acquainted with FitzGerald it does
not seem strange that he did not think of buying
an umbrella or taking a cab. He had planned
the details of his journey and his day in the
city and having settled upon a course of action
a deviation from that course never suggested
itself to him.

George Crabbe said when he was on a visit to
London,—after he had achieved greatness—
where he was received as a genius by the world
of letters: "In my village I am thought nothing
of." And this was true in a marked degree of
FitzGerald. During his lifetime he might well
have said with Crabbe, "In my village I am
thought nothing of." To the people of Woodbridge FitzGerald was an ordinary country

gentleman of eccentric habits. He loved the haphazard, disliking definite engagements, and his greatest enjoyment always came from receiving or paying unexpected visits. He was largely a vegetarian and lived mostly on bread, butter, cheese, porridge, fruit of all kinds and occasionally a raw turnip.

His steadfastness in friendship may be gathered from his letters and his life. Once he made a friend, that person was his friend for life—usually he magnified his virtues, certain it is he was blind to his vices—his friends could do no wrong—that is morally, but FitzGerald was keenly alive to imperfections in their Art and never feared to point them out. He told Tennyson that he should have written nothing after 1842, "leaving Princesses, Ardens, Idylls, etc., all unborn." He ranked Tennyson below " Posh " in real greatness. He says in a letter to Mrs. Kemble that both Tennyson and Thackeray were inferior to " Posh."

One of his boy readers gave me an interesting account of the manner in which FitzGerald spent his evenings when at home.

He, the boy, would arrive about seven o'clock and stay until, perhaps, half-past eight, unless Mr. John Loder happened to look in, when FitzGerald would dismiss him,—somewhat joyfully. He would sit back in his chair and smoke, and would sometimes listen attentively and at other times apparently pay little attention.

He would be attired in dressing-gown and slippers and would take occasional pinches from a snuff-box which he invariably held in his hand. At times he would sit back in his chair and laugh uproariously and at others would become bored and find fault with the reading and reader alike. On such occasions the commencement of the reading of a dry paragraph or a tedious chapter would be met with: " Pass that damned rot ! " or, " What are you reading that for ? " or if it savoured of religious cant, " Read that to my silly brother " (meaning his brother John). He was deeply interested in the " Tichborne Trial " and derisively laughed at the claims of Orton. After the newspaper had been skimmed, would come a chapter from a novel or a biography.

The order of the evening would be occasionally varied by a game of cards—to the delight of the reader. It was in this connection that Mr. Hayward (his boy reader, nicknamed the " Blunderer ") told me of an incident which aptly illustrated FitzGerald's kindness of heart.

One evening when they were playing cards, sitting on either side of the fireplace with the table between them, they were joined by a third party, a mouse, who timorously watched the game for a time from a distance, but gaining courage came forward and stood between the great man and the little boy. FitzGerald held his fingers up to his mouth to signify silence and would on no account have the little creature frightened.

It made its appearance again the next evening, and so on for several successive nights, until it ultimately became so tame that it would feed off crumbs of cake from FitzGerald's hand. It was a source of endless delight to him and he watched for its appearance with much interest, and when upon one occasion the mouse brought a relative to "make up a four" the translator of "Omar" was as happy as a schoolboy.

"Never frighten it away," he would say; "We will sit and watch it, it is like being in prison."

He would get amazing delight out of trivialities. A strange word in the Suffolk vernacular he seized upon with unbounded delight. On one occasion he heard a Woodbridge girl exclaim to a companion in the street, "Where are yer a'goin' to together"—a common Suffolk expression—and for days he could not forget it and repeated it again and again. Regarding another Suffolk word he writes to his friend Mr. Aldis Wright, saying that one Suffolk word had always been an odd mystery to him, "*Dutfin*," a cart bridle—with blinkers—and asking him if he could make anything of it.

A spell of excessively dry or wet weather would try his patience to the utmost, while the cessation of either would be the signal for much jubilation. He suddenly realises that Spring has come and joyfully cries, in his "Meadows in Spring":

> "I jump up like mad,
>   Break the old pipe in twain,
> And away to the meadows,
>   The meadows again."

And in a letter to George Crabbe he remarks that they are expecting rain, but had not had twenty drops for over a month, " though we hear there has been plenty in the Midland Counties. To-day the glass has fallen: and I do think some rain will follow. For the first time I see the long pond at Farlingay all but dry."

It was at the end of this drought that his reader, Arthur Hayward, tells me that he was suddenly stopped in his reading by FitzGerald, after he had just started, by a sharp " Listen! what's that!" The pattering of rain was heard outside. " Shut up the book," cried FitzGerald, " and go home, I'm going out to get soaked!"

On another occasion the " Blunderer" asked, somewhat nervously, if he might have part of an evening off, as he was going to take part in a nigger entertainment. " What?" said FitzGerald, " are you going to be fool enough to black your face?" However, permission was given, but the reader was somewhat disconcerted during the performance to see the form of his master at the back of the room.

FitzGerald's generosity and kindness were constantly being shown by various acts of charity and consideration. The sight of suffering was intolerable to him, and even the recital of a tale of want or of some noble deed always brought the tears to his eyes.

A Woodbridge acquaintance once borrowed a large sum of money (by some said to be £500 and by others £200) and for some time the interest was paid, but soon FitzGerald took the note of hand and put it on the fire, quietly saying, "I think that will do."

Though much of a hermit himself, he liked to see others enjoying themselves, and his grounds would occasionally be thrown open for the benefit of some charity or school-treat. He tells in a letter to Cowell in 1878, how the children of St. John's Parish are coming to play in his grounds, and how he had a large barn cleared in readiness for them, also a swing fixed to a beam. An act of this sort would give FitzGerald great pleasure, it was a part of the ideal life that he craved.

Many of his acts of generosity were never known except to the recipients; he did good by stealth. In writing to Cowell, he thanks him for some partridges, which he says he could have eaten himself if he had not known of a neighbour who was "off her feed," and so he sent them to her. Old soldiers he loved to help, and the fact that a beggar had "fought in Waterloo, sir!" would generally bring its reward in the shape of a dinner or a half-crown.

Another instance of his kindness was told me by the "Blunderer." After being FitzGerald's reader for five or six years he went to a situation in London. One day, when at his work in the shop, he saw a form that he recognised, looking in at the window, a man with a melancholy but proud face, carelessly dressed. "It's my old master, FitzGerald," he said to his fellow assistant, and he ran out and accosted him.

"Who are you?" asked FitzGerald, looking down at him, severely.

"Please sir, the 'Blunderer!'"

FitzGerald's eyes brightened, he made various enquiries as to how he fared in the business and then, thinking it might do the lad a good turn, he went into the shop and spent between five and six pounds, though he really required none of the articles he bought.

Few or none of the writers on Edward FitzGerald have touched upon his humour, perhaps thinking that a man who was so much of a pessimist lacked the humorous perception. But FitzGerald had a keen, if not a discriminating sense of wit; he occasionally punned himself, and at the dinners at Little Grange, when stories were told by Keene, Groome and others, FitzGerald started the laughter and told his tale with the rest. In this, as in many other things, it was the simple tale or joke which amused him most. His housekeeper at Little Grange, Mrs Howe, thus described him: "Such a jokey gentleman he was, too," and she added: "Why, once he said to me, 'Mrs. Howe, I didn't know we had express trains here,' and I said, 'Whatever *do* you mean, sir?' and he says, 'Why, look at Mrs. . . . 's dress there.' And sure enough, she had a long train to it, you know."

His pun about " Old Gooseberry" I have already mentioned. On another occasion FitzGerald had been listening to a long rigmarole from someone in a drawing-room, and the man aired his acquaintance with titled society and told anecdotes about several of his " friends." " Lord So-and-so," " Lady this " and " my friend the Duke." FitzGerald stood it for as long as possible and then left the room, saying as he stood against the door, in a very serious voice, " I too, once knew a Lord, but he is dead."

FitzGerald derived much enjoyment from jokes in which there was little or no real wit, and anecdotes which would fail to raise a smile with everybody else, for some reason would cause him explosions of laughter. His " King of Clubs" (Howe) was once standing bareheaded looking at the pond at Little Grange. "What is it, Howe ? " FitzGerald asked, and the simple " King " replied, " How fond them ducks dew seem of water, to be sure," which was afterwards one of Fitzgerald's, alleged jokes.

He tells his friend Pollock, in a letter in 1872, how he has never guessed a riddle in his life : and so does not even attempt one that Pollock had set him, but he asks Pollock one in return.

THE RIVER DEBEN, WOODBRIDGE.

THE BANKS OF THE DEBEN.
(FitzGerald's favourite walk.)

He writes that at a Christmas party given by a farmer, one of the company, in an inspired moment asked: "Why is Alfred's Christmas tree like the Ipswich Agricultural Show?" and at the end of the letter FitzGerald gives the momentous answer: "Because it is a great success."

Could FitzGerald really have thought this funny or was it merely ironical?

Politics FitzGerald hated. He was a patriot in every sense of the word, but in the region of practical politics he had no place. "Don't write politics," he says, "I agree with you beforehand," a saying that has since become something of an aphorism. In a letter written by Mr. W. B. Donne to Robert H. Groome, the writer says, referring to FitzGerald, "E. F. G. informs me that he gave his landlord instructions in case anyone called about his vote to say that Mr. F. would *not* vote, advised everyone to do the same, and let the rotten matter bust itself." FitzGerald was convinced that England was going to the dogs. He says, "I am quite assured that this country is dying, as other countries die, as trees die, a'top first. The lower limbs are making all haste to follow."

FitzGerald was a dreamer, he walked through life in a dream and to this preoccupation much of his eccentricity was due, and led the Woodbridge folk to apply to him such words as "soft," "mad," "dotty," but it was the madness of genius

—and where is the dividing line? Everyday folk, the conventional, the ordinary folk, have so much taken their own views for granted, and termed them the rational, that any divergence from their own point of view, their own standard, is termed eccentricity and often dubbed "madness." There is a madness which is the *Ultima Thule* of reason.

FitzGerald's strange manner of dress did much to create the impression of "madness."

He walked through the Woodbridge streets wearing an old black-banded tall hat, sometimes tied to his head with a yellow handkerchief, his clothes were untidy and ill-fitting and of cloth of a strange blue colour, short trousers which left several inches of white or grey stockings shewing between their extremities and his loose low shoes, high crumpled collar and carelessly-tied black silk tie, and often a grey plaid shawl about his shoulders. In hot weather he often walked bareheaded and barefooted, with his boots slung across his shoulders or carried on a stick; a strange figure, even in those informal days and in little sleepy Woodbridge, which never made any social pretension. As he walked he moved his head slightly up and down, and often muttered his thoughts aloud or made a kind of hissing noise, sharing this latter habit with his brother John. On one occasion this hissing almost led to the death of his dog. He was walking along the bank of the Deben, his dog at his heels, and lost in thought, and, as the man who told me expressed it, "slightly hissing." He was presently met by a man with a gun, but FitzGerald took no notice, walking on wagging his head and hissing. When the man reached him he suddenly raised his gun to his shoulder and pointed it at the dog, shouting: "You set the dog on me, mister, and I'll shoot him, I will, s'help me!" He imagined that the hissing was an indication or a signal for the dog to "go" for him.

Regarding FitzGerald's habit of absent-mindedness I was told a good story by a man who knew FitzGerald well, and to whom it was told by the man responsible for the incident, FitzGerald's "King of Clubs"!

Howe was well aware of his master's idiosyncrasies, but as he said in his broad Suffolk: "It 'ud never a' done to a' said nothin'."

On one occasion, however, he administered a rebuke to what he termed the "overbearin'" manner of FitzGerald.

It was his duty to keep the lawns and flower-beds at Little Grange in order, and on several occasions he had his attention called to footmarks on the borders and beds which were made by mysterious feet during the night watches. He would leave the beds free from footmarks in the evening but in the morning crushed geraniums and large footprints plainly spoke of a nocturnal intruder. He determined to solve the mystery and to lie in ambush. Accordingly he concealed himself behind a clump of rhododendrons and commenced his vigil.

About ten o'clock a large form loomed in front of him, a form with a plaid shawl over his shoulders, which he at once recognised as his master, Edward FitzGerald. The form paced up and down the paths wrapped in thought. Now he emulated the Persian Poet-Astronomer and gazed up into the star-sprinkled sky; at the same time he stepped back, still looking up, lost in admiration, then further back still, on to flower-beds and borders.

In the morning the handy-man was again admonished. He dared say nothing of his discovery, but that evening he put strong wire round the beds about a foot from the ground and again watched. Once more FitzGerald walked up and down the garden, again he admired the heavens, again he stepped back, until, coming into contact with the wire, he fell full length among mignonette, geraniums and roses. The wire was removed that night and the bed carefully raked over, and though the incident was never mentioned, Howe heard nothing more of trampled flower-beds.

A few months ago I was talking to an old lady in Woodbridge who had lived in that delightful little town for almost eighty years, and I asked her if she had ever seen Edward FitzGerald. She did not remember, where did he live? "On Market Hill," I replied, "for many years, then at Little Grange." "Oh," she answered, "you mean the 'Hare.' Me and my man allus called him the 'Hare.' Yes I've seen him scores of times, both here and at Boulge and 'afore that at Bredfield."

"Why do you call him the 'Hare'?" I asked.

"Well," answered the old lady, "it was like this. Me and my man was going down where Scott's house now stand (the house of the late Seton Merriman), when we see him acomin' along reading a book, with his hat tied on to his head with a handkerchief. He went right past us and instead of turning round towards Melton where the road turn he walks right on, areadin' his book, right into the hedge, and he'd got nearly through afore he knowed it, and a hare, you know, never see right in front, its eyes have been put too far back in its head."

FitzGerald was not a consistent writer, sustained effort was irksome to him, he was indolent and wrote only when he felt like it. In a letter to Bernard Barton, in giving a description of the manner in which he passed his time, he tells how he believes that he will surely be damned for his idle ease.

Yet indolent as he undoubtedly was, the world has cause to be grateful to him for his legacy. All his writings and translations when brought together make a good show, but it must also be remembered that his was a long life and he was in such circumstances that he never had to work for a livelihood. I have briefly referred to some of his favourite works of literature. His own library was not extensive—as libraries of literary men go, but he had access to many libraries, one of them, that of Captain Brooke of Ufford, being what was then perhaps the best private collection of books in the county. He subscribed to the most important papers and magazines of his day and is constantly referring to various articles on current literary matters.

From his letters we can gauge his literary favourites.

Shakespeare he loved. Homer, Plutarch, Æschylus, Pindar, Xenophon and Herodotus, he read and commented upon.

Of the Latin writers he read Lucretius, Seneca, Tacitus, Horace and Virgil, the latter being " one of his loves."

Of Dryden he tells Lowell he cannot tell what is finest, but thinks that Dryden's Prose *quoad* Prose, is the finest style.

Keats, Gray, Lamb and Wordsworth he greatly admired. Lamb more and more, Wordsworth less and less, and Scott he worshipped. Dickens, whom he knew personally, he liked in the same degree that he disliked Browning.

Some of his criticisms of the works of the above-named shew much insight and invariably much delicacy. His criticism is never cutting and seems to lazily creep from his indolent pen.

His religious views were always much of a mystery. With "Omar" he was content to say *Dum vivimus, vivimus*. That he had often pondered over these things is evident from his references thereto in his letters, and he himself once administered a rebuke to a man of the cloth, which shows that he had been seriously concerned over religious matters. A rector of Woodbridge called upon him and expressed his regret that he had never seen him at Church. " Sir," said FitzGerald, " you might have conceived that a man has not come to my years of life without thinking much of these things. I believe I may say that I have reflected on them fully as much as yourself. You need not repeat this visit!" The text on his grave " It is He that hath made us and not we ourselves," which he himself chose, has been quoted as an instance of his orthodoxy, but may there not be an interpretation of the text, that a lover of " Omar Khayyam " might describe thus: As we have not made ourselves but have been made by Him, does not the responsibility rest with Him and not with us?

In his early days he was impressed and much moved by the preaching of the evangelist Matthews of Bedford, but undoubtedly, especially in his latter years, he leaned towards scepticism. He had thought and read and doubtless prayed, but there was a door to which he found no key, he evermore came out by the same door as in he went, but "*He* knows about it all—HE knows—HE knows!" therefore "*Dum spiro, spero!*"

I have a very charitable friend and whenever I, or anyone else anathematises the preacher, she always concludes the argument with the words, "But he is a *good* man." And FitzGerald, whatever his religious beliefs were, was a good man, he was pure-minded, of lofty ideals and noble aspirations. He was loving, loyal and true, generous and charitable. He worshipped the beautiful, but was ever haunted by the idea that it was passing away—dying; his roses bloomed but to die, his harvest was always darkened by the shadow of the sickle :

"Alas, that Spring should vanish with the Rose!
That Youth's sweet-scented Manuscript should close!
The Nightingale that in the Branches sang,
Ah, whence, and whither flown again, who knows?"

He lingered wistfully over the days that were no more, the last Rose of Summer was to him a dirge and not a benediction—it was all passing, passing away; he wrote to Cowell, lamenting that June was over which caused him Omar-like sorrow, the roses were going, always going.

If FitzGerald had never written he would still have been a remarkable man—his friendships with great men would have made him so. He won the respect and love of Carlyle, Tennyson, Thackeray and Spedding among really great men, and of Cowell, Frederick Tennyson,

Bernard Barton, George Crabbe (son of the poet), Mrs. Kemble, John Allen and W. H. Thompson among less known celebrities.

Tennyson loved him best of all his friends, and when asked who was his greatest friend Tennyson would reply, "Why, old Fitz, of course." At the commencement of Tennyson's career FitzGerald almost worshipped him, and over his early poems he was rapturous; but he thought that his work deteriorated in later years, and his disapproval of his poems increased as time went on, but for the man himself he always retained his early love and enthusiasm. In his early days Tennyson was occasionally in need of money, and this knowledge coming to FitzGerald he writes a characteristically generous letter, delicately hinting that he, FitzGerald, would like to give him the money he was in need of.

To be a friend of Carlyle's was assuredly no easy matter, but up to the time of his death FitzGerald was one of the great man's warmest friends, and FitzGerald's admiration for Carlyle's writings increased in the same ratio as they declined in the case of Tennyson. He started by disliking much that Carlyle wrote; to Bernard Barton he writes, of the *French Revolution*, saying " that an Englishman wrote of French Revolutions in a German style, and that though people said the book was deep, it appeared to him only deep because it was written in mystical language; it was scrappy, half reflective, half narrative, and one went through it like a ship goes through a choppy sea."

As he came to know Carlyle better his admiration for his writings increased, for he recognised that what was apparently affectation in Carlyle's style was really a natural mode of expression.

Between the two men an almost continuous correspondence was kept up, and Carlyle evidently came as near to loving FitzGerald as he ever did any man. A " peaceable, affectionate and ultra modest man," Carlyle calls him in a letter to Norton. One of FitzGerald's letters to Carlyle, shewing how often his friend was in his mind, tells of the pleasant evenings he and Carlyle had spent together, of the cups of tea made by "her that is gone," of the pipes they smoked together, of Carlyle's little garden. He tells him that though he did not often write, Carlyle was continually in his thoughts and that reference to one of Carlyle's books prompted him to write his annual letter.

Spedding devoted most of his life to the editing of Bacon's works. He was offered, but declined, the Under-Secretaryship for the Colonies.

As with all his friendships FitzGerald's love for Spedding lasted as long as life itself. Spedding's high, bald forehead was a source of amusement to FitzGerald and Thackeray.

When Spedding was run over by a conveyance in a London street, from the effects of which he died, FitzGerald was much cut up ; he writes to

Aldis Wright of Spedding in sympathetic terms concerning the accident.

Thackeray was, it will be remembered, at Cambridge with FitzGerald, where the two youths —so different in temperament—were chums; and of their trip to Paris I have already spoken. At Cambridge they were constantly in each other's company and amused themselves with writing, sketching and singing.

They were always friends, but FitzGerald does not view him quite as he does his beloved Tennyson, Spedding, or even Carlyle. He doubtless felt it difficult to love Thackeray. FitzGerald, the kindly dreamer, the recluse, fond of quiet country delights and humble joys. Thackeray, full of animal spirits, truly a man of the world, who would probably have laughed at those things which FitzGerald held most sacred, was the antithesis of the gentle FitzGerald, and though he had his portrait hung with that of Tennyson and " Posh," it is certain that in later years they saw little of each other.

His love of his other friends I have sought to make manifest in the chapters devoted to his life, but he had many friends in Woodbridge and the neighbourhood whom I have scarcely mentioned. Mr. John Loder, now a Justice of the Peace for the County, was his firm and constant friend. He it was who occasionally called when FitzGerald's boy readers were performing their allotted task and his visits were esteemed alike by FitzGerald and the boy, by the former on account of the certainty of a pleasant talk with one of his friends and by the latter because it gave him his liberty sooner than he had expected.

Recently I called upon Mr. Loder, and my visit was chosen at a fortunate time, for Mr. Loder had just got together some of his FitzGerald relics, in anticipation of the coming FitzGerald centenary. On the wall was a delightful oil-painting by an Italian master, a present from FitzGerald. From a little drawer he took FitzGerald's watch, of ancient make, in a gold and enamel case of many colours, which was probably the reason FitzGerald chose it. With it was a snuff-box that had likewise been the property of FitzGerald, also with a gaily-coloured picture on its lid. Mr. Loder also showed me a letter from FitzGerald referring to a contemplated re-issue of Moor's *Suffolk Words*.

It will be gathered from the foregoing that FitzGerald longed for affection—his great lonely heart longed for the love of his fellow-men, and he wrote a pathetic letter to Allen, and never did a man write more tenderly, even to the woman he loved, than FitzGerald wrote to his much-loved John Allen. Referring to a letter from Allen he tells how wistfully he had looked for the advent of the letter, how after a walk his eyes turned eagerly to the table to see if it had come. At times, he says, he was tempted to be angry with him, but he was sure that Allen would come a hundred miles to serve him.

FitzGerald had a nickname for everyone and almost everything, even trees and other inanimate objects, had their pseudonyms. His readers were "The Blunderer," on account of his many mistakes, "The Comma," because of his many pauses, "The Ghost," on account of his sudden and punctual appearances at FitzGerald's house. His fisher-captain was "Posh," and his yacht captain "The Magpie." Mr. Howe, his servant at Little Grange, was the "King of Clubs" and "Old Puddle-dog," the latter because of his carelessness. Howe used to rake the cinders out of a stove in the Little Grange hall and did it so noisily that FitzGerald used to sing:

> "Gaily old Puddle-dog
> Banged his guitar."

Charles Keene was "Old Pipes" on account of his love for the bagpipes. Mrs. Howe was the "Fairy Godmother"; the favourite walk in his garden the "Quarter-deck."

During the last few years of his life FitzGerald became more and more enamoured of his beautiful native county of Suffolk. His passion for the haunts of his youth increased. He evidently realised that but little time remained wherein he might look upon the scenes he loved so much. The periods in which he stayed away from Woodbridge became shorter, but his excursions became more frequent, and Lowestoft,

Aldeburgh, Merton, Geldestone, Bury and Beccles, for all of which he had a tender affection, were visited. Eighteen months before his death he writes to his friends of his visits to these places—of a visit to Beccles and gazing on its old Church tower, and going to the house of Mr. Aldis Wright and finding it closed and with drawn blinds.

It is a picture of an old man looking with tear-dimmed eyes on his beautiful past, dreaming again the dreams of his youth—and alone. Friends and things in his letters now become " old " or " dear old." " Dear old Crowfoot," " old Beccles," " old Geldestone " : to Frederick Tennyson my " dear old Friend," and talking about a journey to Merton he talks of taking Cambridge on his way home so that he may see the old place once more for the last time.

Thus was Edward FitzGerald, the dreamer, the hermit, the simple, tender-hearted, pathetic man, whom we Suffolk folk love for his genius, but more for his beautiful character, and for the legacy he has left us, and still more because he first loved us and our sleepy but beautiful old towns and villages, and by his sojourn in them gave them an added lustre and a fresh charm.

To his virtues, it would be superfluous to be kind and he had few faults to beg blindness of our charity. " His life was gentle and the elements so mixed in him that nature might stand up and say to all the world—'this was a man.' "

CHAPTER VII.

WORKS.

The literary output of Edward FitzGerald was not prodigious, and probably in his bibliography there is little that has in it the stuff of immortality. " Omar," of course, will live. It has taken its place in the literary firmament as one of the brightest stars, and by its genius has placed Edward FitzGerald among the prophets. But it may be urged that " Omar " is not an original work, and this is correct, but " Omar " without FitzGerald, it is safe to assert, would ever have remained in oblivion, or at most, would have had an exceedingly limited number of readers and less admirers. Of the original works of FitzGerald, his letters and one or two poems, with here and there a fine passage of prose, display the genius of the translator of " Omar," but the remainder of his works are mediocre.

His bibliography, in chronological order, is as follows :

    1831 The Meadows in Spring.
           Will Thackeray.
    1832 Canst Thou, My Clora ?
    1833 On Annie Allen.
           ' The Old Beau.'
    1839 Bredfield Hall.

1841	Chronomoros.
1847	Notes to the "Table Talk of John Selden."
1849	Memoir to Bernard Barton.
1851	Euphranor.
1852	Polonius.
1853	Six Dramas from Calderon.
1855	Euphranor (Second Edition).
1856	Salaman and Absal.
	Attar's "Bird Parliament."
1859	Omar Khayyam.
1860 & 1861	"F." Articles to *East Anglian Daily Times*. "Parathina" contributions to *Notes and Queries*.
1862	Virgil's Garden
	Omar Khayyam (reprint)
1865	Magico and Such Stuff as Dreams are made of.
	Agamemnon
1868	Two Generals.
	Omar Khayyam (2nd Edition).
1868 to 1870	"E. F. G." Articles to *East Anglian Daily Times*.
1871	Salaman and Absal (2nd Edition).
1872	Omar Khayyam (3rd Edition).
1876	Agamemnon (2nd Edition).
1877 & 1878	"Effigy" Articles to *East Anglian Daily Times*. Notes on Charles Lamb.
1879	Salaman and Absal (3rd Edition).
	Omar Khayyam (4th Edition).
	Readings in Crabbe.
1880	Articles in *Temple Bar*.
1880 & 1881	Œdipus
1882	Virgil's Garden.
	Euphranor (3rd Edition)

In addition to the above FitzGerld wrote some

notes to *Wesley's Journal* which have been lost, but may some day be re-discovered, in which event their publication would be of much interest. FitzGerald often quoted Wesley and his *Journal* was among his favourite books.

His first poem, published in Hone's *Year Book* in 1831, was the charming " Meadows in Spring," a lyric, beautiful in sentiment and admirable in construction.

THE MEADOWS IN SPRING.

" 'Tis a dull sight
   To see the year dying,
When winter winds
   Set the yellow wood sighing :
   Sighing, oh! sighing.

" When such a time cometh,
   I do retire
Into an old room
   Beside a bright fire :
   Oh, pile a bright fire !

" And there I sit
   Reading old things,
Of knights and lorn damsels
   While the wind sings—
   Oh, drearily sings !

" I never look out
   Nor attend to the blast ;
For all to be seen
   Is the leaves falling fast :
   Falling, falling !

"But close at the hearth,
 Like a cricket, sit I,
Reading of summer
 And chivalry—
Gallant chivalry!

"Then with an old friend
 I talk of our youth—
How 'twas gladsome, but often
 Foolish, forsooth :
But gladsome, gladsome!

"Or to get merry
 We sing some old rhyme,
That made the wood ring again
 In summer time—
Sweet summer time!

"Then go we to smoking,
 Silent and snug :
Nought passes between us,
 Save a brown jug—
Sometimes!

"And sometimes a tear
 Will rise in each eye
Seeing the two old friends
 So merrily—so merrily!

"And ere to bed
 Go we, go we,
Down on the ashes,
 We kneel on the knee,
Praying together!

"Thus, then, live I,
 Till 'mid all the gloom,
By Heaven! the bold sun
 Is with me in the room
Shining, shining!

> "Then the clouds part,
>   Swallows soaring between,
> The Spring is alive,
>   And the meadows are green!"
>
> "I jump up like mad,
>   Break the old pipe in twain,
> And away to the Meadows,
>   The Meadows again!"

This lyric, so sweetly tender, with its lights and shades and its quiet easy-flowing rhythm, was written when FitzGerald was only twenty-two, and it bears evidences of that retrospective sadness which even in those early days had tinged his life. The last line of each stanza, with its haunting refrain, is wistful in the extreme. In the eighth stanza he approaches the humorous with "Nought passes between us save a brown jug"—and its sly one-word last line "Sometimes!" but he at once smothers it and gets back to pathos in the next verse. Suddenly, in the midst of his musings of dark winter, he realises the sun has come back, that the Spring is alive, the meadows green, and:

> "I jump up like mad,
>   Break the old pipe in twain,
> And away to the Meadows,
>   The Meadows again."

The world would have been thankful for more of this sylvan, lyric song, and when we consider FitzGerald's love of simple country scenes and nature generally it is perhaps strange that he wrote so little in a similar strain.

The next year he wrote those beautiful verses "To a Lady Singing." Many think that he had Annie Allen in mind when writing them.

TO A LADY SINGING.

" Can'st thou, my Clora, declare,
  After thy sweet song dieth
Into the wild summer air,
  Whither it falleth or flieth?
Soon would my answer be noted
Wert thou but sage as sweet-throated.

" Melody, dying away,
  Into the dark sky closes,
Like the good soul from her clay,
  Like the fair odour of roses;
Therefore thou now art behind it,
But thou shalt follow, and find it.

" Nothing can utterly die:
  Music aloft up-springing
Turns to pure atoms of sky
  Each golden note of thy singing:
And that to which morning did listen
At eve in a rainbow may glisten.

" Beauty when laid in the grave
  Feedeth the lily beside her,
Therefore the soul cannot have
  Station or honour denied her;
She will not better her essence,
But wear a crown in God's presence."

The last two verses were added at a later date. The poem is one of singular beauty, especially the first three verses, and it is cause for wonder that no composer has—so far as I know—ever set them to music. The fanciful idea in the third verse of the golden notes of the singer ascending to the heavens in the morning to scintillate in the evening rainbow, is as charming as it is original. The last verse certainly does not improve the poem, the ideal ending is the last line of the third verse.

"The Old Beau" appeared in *The Keepsake* in 1834. It is in many respects a fine poem reminiscent of the old English ballads, written in a jaunty style, the kind of thing one would go a-hunting to. An old Beau reviews his life and laments modern decadence:

"The days we used to laugh, Tom,
At tales of love, and tears of passion;
The bowls we used to quaff, Tom,
In toasting all the toasts in fashion;
The heaths and hills we ranged, Tom,
When limb ne'er fail'd, when step ne'er falter'd;
Alas! how things are changed, Tom,
How we—and all the world—are alter'd.

The complete poem contains ten eight-lined verses, in which the Beau describes his College days, how now even the climate has grown several degrees colder and the world is fast hastening towards dissolution.

"The world, I oft suspect, Tom,
Draws near its close; and isn't it better
To die, when no respect, Tom,
Is shown from creditor to debtor?
When tradesfolk make a row, Tom,

A year or two if you delay them,
  And often ask you now, Tom,
With perfect *nonchalance*, to pay them?"

"Bredfield Hall" was written in 1839, and is, but for one or two slight metrical faults, a very fine poem in the Tennyson style. It is a kind of panorama of events, the scene being laid at his birthplace, Bredfield Hall (now called "Bredfield House" and at the time of his birth the "White House").

On several occasions I have visited Bredfield House, which stands on high ground about a mile and a half outside Woodbridge. From the highest point may be seen the waters of Hollesley (called Hosely) Bay where, as mentioned in the poem, Nelson's fleet anchored after its return from Trafalgar, and a delightful view of the surrounding country may be obtained.

The poem is so good, and so little known, that I give it in full:

BREDFIELD HALL.

"Lo, an English mansion founded
  In the elder James's reign,
Quaint and stately, and surrounded
  With a pastoral domain.

With well-timber'd lawn and gardens
  And with many a pleasant mead,
Skirted by the lofty coverts
  Where the hare and pheasant feed.

Flank'd it is with goodly stables,
  Shelter'd by coeval trees:

So it lifts its honest gables
　　Toward the distant German Seas;

Where it once discern'd the smoke
　　Of old sea-battles far away:
Saw victorious Nelson's topmasts
　　Anchoring in Hollesley Bay.

But whatever storm might riot,
　　Cannon roar, and trumpet ring,
Still amid these meadows quiet
　　Did the yearly violet spring:

Still Heaven's starry hand suspended
　　That light balance of the dew,
That each night on earth descended,
　　And each morning rose anew:

And the ancient house stood rearing
　　Undisturb'd her chimneys high,
And her gilded vanes still veering
　　Toward each quarter of the sky:

While like wave to wave succeeding
　　Through the world of joy and strife,
Household after household speeding,
　　Handed on the torch of life:

First, Sir Knight in ruff and doublet,
　　Arm in arm with stately dame;
Then the Cavaliers indignant
　　For their monarch brought to shame:

Languid beauties limn'd by Lely;
　　Full-wigg'd Justice of Queen Anne:
Tory squires who tippled freely;
　　And the modern Gentleman:

Here they lived, and here they greeted,
　　Maids and matrons, sons and sires,
Wandering in its walks, or seated
　　Round its hospitable fires:

Oft their silken dresses floated
  Gleaming through the pleasure ground:
Oft dash'd by the scarlet-coated
  Hunter, horse, and dappled hound.

Till the Bell that not in vain
  Had summon'd them to weekly prayer,
Call'd them one by one again
  To the church—and left them there!

They with all their loves and passions,
  Compliment, and song, and jest,
Politics, and sports, and fashions,
  Merged in everlasting rest!

So they pass—while thou, old Mansion,
  Markest with unalter'd face
How like the foliage of thy summers
  Race of man succeeds to race.

To most thou stand'st a record sad,
  But all the sunshine of the year
Could not make thine aspect glad
  To one whose youth is buried here.

In thine ancient rooms and gardens
  Buried—and his own no more
Than the youth of those old owners,
  Dead two centuries before.

Unto him the fields around thee
  Darken with the days gone by:
O'er the solemn woods that bound thee
  Ancient sunsets seem to die.

Sighs the self-same breeze of morning
  Through the cypress as of old;
Ever at the Spring's returning
  One same crocus breaks the mould.

> Still though 'scaping Time's more savage
>   Handywork this pile appears,
> It has not escaped the ravage
>   Of the undermining years.
>
> And though each succeeding master,
>   Grumbling at the cost to pay,
> Did with coat of paint and plaster
>   Hide the wrinkles of decay;
>
> Yet the secret worm ne'er ceases,
>   Nor the mouse behind the wall;
> Heart of oak will come to pieces,
>   And farewell to Bredfield Hall!"

In 1851 appeared the first edition of *Euphranor* which FitzGerald, not thinking a great deal of, called "a pretty specimen of a chiselled cherry-stone," though this does not give a particularly lucid idea of *Euphranor*, a "chiselled cherry-stone" being a mystery understood by few. What he probably wished to convey was that it was a small work delicately executed. The *Euphranor* is a beautiful piece of Plato-like writing in fine but simple English. Four Cambridge undergraduates, Euphranor, the hero, an impulsive, enthusiastic, hot-headed youth; Lycion, a generous, indolent fop; Phidippus, a warm and simple-hearted Esau (drawn from FitzGerald's friend W. K. Brown), and Lexilogus, of giant intellect, but humble and ingenuous. The narrator, a Cambridge physician, is an elderly, sobered kind of guardian of the youths.

Euphranor consists largely of the discussions of the quintette; they talk of chivalry, education, literature, sport, etc., and in these talks are some charming passages, especially in the references to Tennyson. The little work is full of a sweet poetical spirit, permeated with the FitzGerald pathetic wail of the ever-passing happiness.

One of the finest parts is the description of the Boat-race:

THE BOAT-RACE, FROM *Euphranor*.

" Shortly after this, the rest of us agreed it was time to be gone. We walked along the fields by the Church (purposely to ask about the sick Lady by the way), cross'd the Ferry, and mingled with the crowd upon the opposite shore; Townsmen and Gownsmen, with the tassell'd Fellow-commoner sprinkled here and there—Reading men and Sporting men—Fellows, and even Masters of Colleges, not indifferent to the prowess of their respective Crews—all these, conversing on all sorts of topics, from the slang in *Bell's Life* to the last new German Revelation, and moving in ever-changing groups down the shore of the river, at whose farther bend was a little knot of ladies gathered up on a green knoll faced and illuminated by the beams of the setting sun. Beyond which point was at length heard some indistinct shouting, which gradually increased, until ' They are off—they are coming!' suspended our conversation among ourselves; and suddenly the head of the first boat turn'd the corner : and then another close upon it ; and then a third ; the crews pulling with all their might compacted into perfect rhythm ; and the crowd on shore turning round to follow along with them, waving hats and caps, and cheering, ' Bravo, St. John's ! Go it, Trinity ! '—the high crest and blowing forelock of Phidippus's mare, and he himself shouting encouragement to his crew, conspicuous over all—until, the boats reaching us, we also were caught up in the returning tide of spectators, and hurried back towards the goal ; where we arrived just in time to see the Ensign of Trinity lowered from its pride of place, and the eagle of St. John's soaring there instead. Then, waiting a little while to hear how the winner had won and the loser lost, and watching Phidippus engaged in eager conversation with his defeated brethren, I took Euphranor and Lexilogus under either arm (Lycion having got into better company elsewhere), and walked home with them across the meadow leading to the town, whither the dusky troops of Gownsmen with all their confused voices seem'd, as it were, evaporating in the twilight, while a nightingale began to be heard among the flowering chestnuts of Jesus."

Polonius, a Collection of Wise Saws and Modern Instances, appeared in 1852. It consists, as the title suggests, of a number of aphorisms and selections, many of them of some considerable length, from the works of Carlyle,

Bacon, Selden, Milton, Scott, Goethe, etc., Carlyle largely predominating. The preface contains some delightful passages :

"When Sir Walter Scott lay dying, he called for his son-in-law, and while the Tweed murmured through the woods, and a September sun lit up the towers, whose growth he had watched so eagerly, said to him, "Be a good man ; only that can comfort you when you come to lie here!" "*Be a good man !*"

"To that threadbare truism shrunk all that gorgeous tapestry of written and real romance!"

"You knew all this," wrote Johnson to Mrs. Thrale, rallying for a little while from his final attack—"You knew all this, and I thought I knew it too ; but I know it now with a new conviction."

"Perhaps, next to realising all this in our own lives (when just too late), we become most sensible of it in reading the lives and deaths of others, such as Scott's and Johnson's ; when we see all the years of life, with all their ambitions, loves, animosities, schemes of action—all the *" curas supervacuas, spes inanes, et inexspectatos exitus hujus fugacissimae vitae "*—summed up in a volume or two ; and what seemed so long a history to them, but a Winter's Tale to us."

"Death itself was no truism to Adam and Eve, nor to many of their successors, I suppose : nay, some of their very latest descendants, it is said, have doubted if it be an inevitable necessity of life: others, with more probability, whether a man can fully comprehend its inevitableness till life itself be half over ; beginning to believe he must die about the same time he begins to believe he is a fool."

> "As are the leaves on the trees, even so are man's generations ;
> This is the truest verse ever a poet has sung:
> Nevertheless few hearing it hear; Hope, flattering alway,
> Lives in the bosom of all—reigns in the blood of the Young."

The following also is very fine :

"And why," says the note-book of one *nel mezzo del cammin di nostra vita*, " does one day linger in my memory ? I had started one fine October morning on a ramble through the villages that lie beside the Ouse. In high health and cloudless spirits, one regret perhaps hanging upon the horizon of the heart, I walked through Sharnbrook up the hill, and paused by the church on the summit to look about me. The sun shone, the clouds flew, the yellow trees shook in the wind, the river rippled in breadths of light and dark ; rooks and daws wheeled and cawed aloft in the changing spaces of blue above the spire ; the churchyard all still in the sunshine below."

Polonius was followed, in 1853, by the *Six Dramas from Calderon*, consisting of a translation or adaptation of six Spanish plays by Calderon. In 1855 came a second edition of *Euphranor*, followed in 1856 by *Salaman and Absal*.

Jami, the author of *Salaman and Absal*, was a Persian poet who was born in 1414 and died in 1492. He attended the great Samarcand School, but went back to Herat, called hither, he said, by a dream. He joined the strange Sufi sect and lived a solitary philosophical life, but the Muse compelled him to write poetry, and in addition he wrote a great number of volumes on theology, grammar, etc.

Salaman and Absal is an allegory and FitzGerald translated the poem into blank verse, and the incidents into a sparkling unrhymed metre.

Briefly the story is this: The Shah of Yunan invokes heaven for a son, and in answer to his prayers a beautiful and gifted child, Salaman, is given him. Absal, a young and beautiful girl, becomes the foster-mother of the divine Salaman, and as the child grows to manhood he falls in love with her, and devotes all his time at her shrine.

Being rebuked by the Shah, he flies with Absal to the desert and from thence on a boat with magic properties to a fair isle of Paradise. For a time they dwell here, until Salaman, awaking from his dream and full of contrition, returns to his father. But his old passion returns and not being able to decide 'twixt love and duty, he decides to die with Absal. Together they fling themselves in a fire and Absal perishes, but Salaman being protected by magical arts is preserved.

As in many of his other translations, the work of FitzGerald in this poem is good in parts. Taken as a whole the story is wearisome, but such passages as the following, which is a description of the sea upon which Salaman and Absal sail to the beautiful island, rescue it from mediocrity :

> "He halted on the Seashore; on the shore
> Of a great Sea that reaching like a floor
> Of rolling firmament below the Skies
> From Kaf to Kaf, to Gau and Mahi down
> Descended, and its Stars were living eyes.
> The Face of it was as it were a range
> Of moving Mountains; or a countless host
> Of Camels trooping tumultuously up,
> Host over host, and foaming at the lip.
> Within, innumerable glittering things
> Sharp as cut Jewels, to the sharpest eye
> Scarce visible, hither and hither slipping,
> As silver scissors slice a blue brocade."

Attar's *Bird Parliament* came in the next year, 1856, and like *Salaman and Absal* is an adaptation. Its author, Farid-Uddin Attar, was also a Persian poet, born in 1119.

The Birds meet together to select a King and each states his claim to sovereignty. The Tajidar is finally chosen and after his oration on the search for the author of life a band of birds set out on a pilgrimage to discover the mystery of life and many, under the lead of Tajidar, ultimately gaze on the vision of God.

FitzGerald's translation bears the marks of

infinite care, but it savours so strongly of the Oriental, that to the average reader it is confusing.

FitzGerald's next work was his masterpiece, the immortal *Rubaiyat*, the first edition of which he published at his own expense in 1859.

Viewed in the light of its present-day popularity, when it is selling in its thousands, it appears well-nigh inconceivable that the *Rubaiyat* suffered the fate of many of the world's masterpieces and was practically a rejected MS.

If it was not actually returned to FitzGerald accompanied by the polite little rejection note: " The Editor presents his compliments to the writer of the enclosed MS., the *Rubaiyat of Omar Khayyam*, and regrets that he is unable to avail himself of the use of it," the fact remains that FitzGerald sent it to *Fraser's Magazine* and twelve months later, as it had not been used, he wrote for its return.

FitzGerald had two hundred and fifty copies printed and he sent a few to his various friends, and as the others failed to sell, he gave them to Mr. Quaritch, who put them in his " twopenny box," indeed, many of them were sold for 1*d.*—to-day they are worth £30.

Before saying anything more about the *Rubaiyat* we will give the poem itself:

BOULGE CHURCH.
(The FitzGerald mausoleum is on the left of the tower.)
Photo. Welton, Woodbridge.

BOULGE COTTAGE.
Photo. Welton, Woodbridge.

RUBÁIYÁT OF OMAR KHAYYÁM.

As Interpreted by Edward FitzGerald.

I

Awake! for Morning in the Bowl of Night.
Has flung the Stone that puts the Stars to Flight:
   And Lo! the Hunter of the East has caught
The Sultán's Turret in a Noose of Light.

II

Dreaming when Dawn's Left Hand was in the Sky
I heard a Voice within the Tavern cry,
   "Awake, my Little ones, and fill the Cup
Before Life's Liquor in its Cup be dry."

III

And, as the Cock crew, those who stood before
The Tavern shouted—"Open then the Door!
   You know how little while we have to stay,
And, once departed, may return no more."

IV

Now the New Year reviving old Desires,
The thoughtful Soul to Solitude retires,
   Where the WHITE HAND OF MOSES on the Bough
Puts out, and Jesus from the Ground suspires.

V

Irám indeed is gone with all its Rose,
And Jamshýd's Sev'n-ring'd Cup where no one knows;
   But still the Vine her ancient Ruby yields,
And still a Garden by the Water blows.

VI

And David's Lips are lockt; but in divine
High piping Pehleví, with "Wine! Wine! Wine!
Red Wine!"—the Nightingale cries to the Rose
That yellow Cheek of her's to incarnadine.

VII

Come, fill the Cup, and in the Fire of Spring
The Winter Garment of Repentance fling:
    The Bird of Time has but a little way
To fly—and Lo! the Bird is on the Wing.

VIII

And look—a thousand Blossoms with the Day
Woke—and a thousand scatter'd into Clay:
    And this first Summer Month that brings the Rose
Shall take Jamshýd and Kaikobád away.

IX

But come with old Khayyám, and leave the Lot
Of Kaikobád and Kaikhosrú forgot:
    Let Rustum lay about him as he will,
Or Hátim Tai cry Supper—heed them not.

X

With me along some Strip of Herbage strown
That just divides the desert from the sown,
    Where name of Slave and Sultán scarce is known,
And pity Sultán Mahmúd on his Throne.

XI

Here with a Loaf of Bread beneath the Bough,
A Flask of Wine, a Book of Verse—and Thou
    Beside me singing in the Wilderness—
And Wilderness is Paradise enow.

XII

" How sweet is mortal Sovranty ! "—think some:
Others—" How blest the Paradise to come! "
 Ah, take the Cash in hand and waive the Rest;
Oh, the brave Music of a *distant* Drum!

XIII

Look to the Rose that blows about us—"Lo,
Laughing," she says, " into the World I blow :
 At once the silken Tassel of my Purse
Tear, and its Treasure on the Garden throw."

XIV

The Worldly Hope men set their Hearts upon
Turns Ashes—or it prospers ; and anon,
 Like Snow upon the Desert's dusty Face
Lighting a little Hour or two—is gone.

XV

And those who husbanded the Golden Grain,
And those who flung it to the Winds like Rain,
 Alike to no such aureate Earth are turn'd
As, buried once, Men want dug up again.

XVI

Think, in this batter'd Caravanserai
Whose Doorways are alternate Night and Day,
 How Sultán after Sultán with his Pomp
Abode his Hour or two, and went his way.

XVII

They say the Lion and the Lizard keep
The Courts where Jamshýd gloried and drank deep ;
 And Bahrám, that great Hunter—the Wild Ass
Stamps o'er his Head, and he lies fast asleep.

XVIII

I sometimes think that never blows so red
The Rose as where some buried Cæsar bled;
  That every Hyacinth the Garden wears
Dropt in its Lap from some once lovely Head.

XIX

And this delightful Herb whose tender Green
Fledges the River's Lip on which we lean—
  Ah, lean upon it lightly! for who knows
From what once lovely Lip it springs unseen!

XX

Ah, my Belovéd, fill the Cup that clears
To-DAY of past Regrets and future Fears—
  To-morrow?—Why, To-morrow I may be
Myself with Yesterday's Sev'n Thousand Years.

XXI

Lo! some we loved, the loveliest and best
That Time and Fate of all their Vintage prest,
  Have drunk their Cup a Round or two before,
And one by one crept silently to Rest.

XXII.

And we, that now make merry in the Room
They left, and Summer dresses in new Bloom,
  Ourselves must we beneath the Couch of Earth
Descend, ourselves to make a Couch—for whom?

XXIII

Ah, make the most of what we yet may spend,
Before we too into the Dust descend;
  Dust into Dust, and under Dust, to lie,
Sans Wine, sans Song, sans Singer, and—sans End!

XXIV

Alike for those who for To-DAY prepare,
And those that after a To-MORROW stare,
  A Muezzin from the Tower of Darkness cries
" Fools! your Reward is neither Here nor There!"

XXV

Why, all the Saints and Sages who discuss'd
Of the Two Worlds so learnedly, are thrust
  Like foolish Prophets forth; their Words to Scorn
Are scatter'd, and their Mouths are stopt with Dust.

XXVI

Oh, come with old Khayyám, and leave the Wise
To talk; one thing is certain, that Life flies;
  One thing is certain, and the Rest is Lies;
The Flower that once has blown for ever dies.

XXVII

Myself when young did eagerly frequent
Doctor and Saint, and heard great Argument
  About it and about: but evermore
Came out by the same Door as in I went.

XXVIII

With them the Seed of Wisdom did I sow,
And with my own hand labour'd it to grow:
  And this was all the Harvest that I reap'd—
" I came like Water, and like Wind I go."

XXIX

Into this Universe, and *why* not knowing,
Nor *whence*, like Water willy-nilly flowing:
  And out of it, as Wind along the Waste,
I know not *whither*, willy-nilly blowing.

XXX

What, without asking, hither hurried *whence?*
And, without asking, *whither* hurried hence!
  Another and another Cup to drown
The Memory of this Impertinence!

XXXI

Up from Earth's Centre through the Seventh Gate
I rose, and on the Throne of Saturn sate,
  And many Knots unravel'd by the Road;
But not the Knot of Human Death and Fate.

XXXII

There was a Door to which I found no Key:
There was a Veil past which I could not see:
  Some little Talk awhile of ME and THEE
There seem'd—and then no more of THEE and ME.

XXXIII

Then to the rolling Heav'n itself I cried,
Asking, " What Lamp had Destiny to guide
  Her little Children stumbling in the Dark?"
And—" A blind understanding!"—Heav'n replied.

XXXIV

Then to this earthen Bowl did I adjourn
My Lip the secret Well of Life to learn:
  And Lip to Lip it murmur'd—" While you live
Drink!—for once dead you never shall return."

XXXV

I think the Vessel, that with fugitive
Articulation answer'd, once did live,
  And merry-make; and the cold Lip I kiss'd
How many Kisses might it take—and give!

XXXVI

For in the Market-place, one Dusk of Day,
I watch'd the Potter thumping his wet Clay:
   And with its all obliterated Tongue
It murmur'd—"Gently, Brother, gently, pray!"

XXXVII

Ah, fill the Cup:—what boots it to repeat
How Time is slipping underneath our Feet:
   Unborn To-MORROW, and dead YESTERDAY,
Why fret about them if To-DAY be sweet!

XXXVIII

One Moment in Annihilation's Waste,
One Moment, of the Well of Life to taste—
   The Stars are setting and the Caravan
Starts for the Dawn of Nothing—Oh, make haste!

XXXIX

How long, how long, in infinite Pursuit
Of This and That endeavour and dispute?
   Better be merry with the fruitful Grape
Than sadden after none, or bitter, Fruit.

XL

You know, my Friends, how long since in my House
For a new Marriage I did make Carouse:
   Divorced old barren Reason from my Bed,
And took the Daughter of the Vine to Spouse.

XLI

For "Is" and "Is-NOT" though *with* Rule and Line,
And "Up-AND-DOWN" *without*, I could define,
   I yet in all I only cared to know,
Was never deep in anything but—Wine.

XLII

And lately, by the Tavern Door agape,
Came stealing through the Dusk an Angel Shape
  Bearing a Vessel on his Shoulder; and
He bid me taste of it; and 'twas—the Grape.

XLIII

The Grape that can with Logic absolute
The Two-and-Seventy jarring Sects confute:
  The subtle Alchemist that in a Trice
Life's leaden Metal into Gold transmute.

XLIV

The mighty Mahmúd, the victorious Lord,
That all the misbelieving and black Horde
  Of Fears and Sorrows that infest the Soul,
Scatters and slays with his enchanted Sword.

XLV

But leave the Wise to wrangle, and with me
The Quarrel of the Universe let be:
  And, in some corner of the Hubbub coucht,
Make Game of that which makes as much of Thee.

XLVI

For in and out, above, about, below,
'Tis nothing but a Magic Shadow-show,
  Play'd in a Box whose Candle is the Sun,
Round which we Phantom Figures come and go.

XLVII

And if the Wine you drink, the Lip you press,
End in the Nothing all Things end in—Yes—
  Then fancy while Thou art, Thou art but what
Thou shalt be—Nothing—Thou shalt not be less.

XLVIII

While the Rose blows along the River Brink,
With old Khayyám the Ruby Vintage drink:
   And when the Angel with his darker Draught
Draws up to Thee—take that, and do not shrink.

XLIX

'Tis all a Chequer-board of Nights and Days
Where Destiny with Men for Pieces plays:
   Hither and thither moves, and mates and slays,
And one by one back in the Closet lays.

L

The Ball no Question makes of Ayes and Noes,
But Right or Left as strikes the Player goes;
   And He that toss'd Thee down into the Field,
He knows about it all—HE knows—HE knows!

LI

The Moving Finger writes; and, having writ,
Moves on: nor all thy Piety nor Wit
   Shall lure it back to cancel half a Line,
Nor all thy Tears wash out a Word of it.

LII

And that inverted Bowl we call The Sky,
Whereunder crawling coopt we live and die,
   Lift not thy hands to *It* for help—for It
Rolls impotently on as Thou or I.

LIII

With Earth's first Clay They did the Last Man's knead,
And then of the Last Harvest sow'd the Seed:
   Yea, the first Morning of Creation wrote
What the Last Dawn of Reckoning shall read.

LIV

I tell Thee this—When, starting from the Goal,
Over the shoulders of the flaming Foal
   Of Heav'n Parwín and Mushtara they flung,
In my predestin'd Plot of Dust and Soul

LV

The Vine had struck a Fibre; which about
If clings my Being—let the Súfi flout;
   Of my Base Metal may be filed a Key,
That shall unlock the Door he howls without.

LVI

And this I know: whether the one True Light,
Kindle to Love, or Wrath consume me quite,
   One glimpse of It within the Tavern caught
Better than in the Temple lost outright.

LVII

Oh, Thou, who didst with Pitfall and with Gin
Beset the Road I was to wander in,
   Thou wilt not with Predestination round
Enmesh me, and impute my Fall to Sin?

LVIII

Oh, Thou, who Man of baser Earth didst make,
And who with Eden didst devise the Snake;
   For all the Sin wherewith the Face of Man
Is blacken'd, Man's Forgiveness give—and take!

KÚZA-NÁMA

LIX

Listen again. One evening at the Close
Of Ramazán, ere the better Moon arose,
   In that old Potter's Shop I stood alone
With the clay Population round in Rows.

LX

And, strange to tell, among that Earthern Lot
Some could articulate, while others not :
 And suddenly one more impatient cried—
"Who *is* the Potter, pray, and who the Pot?"

LXI

Then said another—" Surely not in vain
My Substance from the common Earth was ta'en,
 That He who subtly wrought me into Shape
Should stamp me back to common Earth again."

LXII

Another said—" Why ne'er a peevish Boy,
Would break the Bowl from which he drank in Joy;
 Shall He that *made* the Vessel in pure Love
And Fancy, in an after Rage destroy!"

LXIII

None answer'd this; but after Silence spake
A Vessel of a more ungainly Make :
 "They sneer at me for leaning all awry;
What! did the Hand then of the Potter shake?"

LXIV

Said one—" Folks of a surly Tapster tell,
And daub his Visage with the Smoke of Hell;
 They talk of some strict Testing of us—Pish!
He's a Good Fellow, and t'will all be well."

LXV

Then said another with a long-drawn Sigh,
"My Clay with long oblivion is gone dry :
 But, fill me with the old familiar Juice,
Methinks I might recover by-and-bye!"

LXVI

So while the Vessels one by one were speaking,
One spied the little Crescent all were seeking:
   And then they jogg'd each other, "Brother! Brother!
Hark to the Porter's Shoulder-knot a-creaking!"

LXVII

Ah, with the Grape my fading Life provide,
And wash my Body whence the Life has died,
   And in a Windingsheet of Vine-leaf wrapt,
So bury me by some sweet Garden-side.

LXVIII

That ev'n my buried Ashes such a Snare
Of Perfume shall fling up into the Air,
   As not a True Believer passing by
But shall be overtaken unaware.

LXIX

Indeed the Idols I have loved so long
Have done my Credit in Men's Eye much wrong:
   Have drown'd my Honour in a shallow Cup,
And sold my Reputation for a Song.

LXX

Indeed, indeed, Repentance oft before
I swore—but was I sober when I swore?
   And then and then came Spring, and Rose-in-hand
My thread-bare Penitence apieces tore.

LXXI

And much as Wine has play'd the Infidel,
And robb'd me of my Robe of Honour—well,
   I often wonder what the Vintners buy
One half so precious as the Goods they sell.

LXXII

Alas, that Spring should vanish with the Rose!
That Youth's sweet-scented Manuscript should close!
 The Nightingale that in the Branches sang,
Ah, whence, and whither flown again, who knows!

LXXIII

Ah Love! could thou and I with Fate conspire
To grasp this sorry Scheme of Things entire,
 Would not we shatter it to bits—and then
Re-mould it nearer to the Heart's Desire!

LXXIV

Ah, Moon of my Delight who know'st no wane,
The Moon of Heav'n is rising once again:
 How oft hereafter rising shall she look
Through this same Garden after me—in vain!

LXXV

And when Thyself with shining Foot shall pass
Among the Guests Star-scatter'd on the Grass,
 And in thy joyous Errand reach the Spot
Where I made one—turn down an empty Glass!

TAMAM SHUD

Omar Khayyam, the Persian poet, was born at Naishapur, in Khorassan, about the middle of the eleventh century, and died in 1123; his tomb may still be seen at Naishapur.

Two other men, both great men in their day, Hasan al Sabbah and Nizam al Mulk, were his youthful friends, and they all studied at

Naishapur, under Abd-u-Samad, a man of great learning and a doctor of law.

The second of these youths, Nizam al Mulk, in his Wasyat or *Testament* relates the story of the three, which appears in the preface to the first edition of the "Omar." He says:

"One of the greatest of the wise men of Khorassan was the Imam Mowaffak of Naishapur, a man highly honoured and reverenced,—may God rejoice his soul; his illustrious years exceeded eighty-five, and it was the universal belief that every boy who read the Koran, or studied the traditions in his presence, would assuredly attain to honour and happiness. For this cause did my father send me from Tus to Naishapur with Abd-u-Samad, the doctor of law, that I might employ myself in study and learning under the guidance of that illustrious teacher. Towards me he ever turned an eye of favour and kindness, and as his pupil I felt for him extreme affection and devotion, so that I passed four years in his service. When I first came there, I found two other pupils of mine own age newly arrived, Hakim Omar Khayyam and the ill-fated Ben Sabbah. Both were endowed with sharpness of wit and the highest natural powers; and we three formed a close friendship together. When the Imam rose from his lectures, they used to join me, and we repeated to each other the lessons we had heard. Now Omar was a native of Naishapur, while Hasan Ben Sabbah's father was one Ali, a man of austere life and practice, but heretical in his creed and doctrine. One day Hasan said to me and to Khayyam, 'It is a universal belief that the pupils of the Imam Mowaffak will attain to fortune. Now even if we *all* do not attain thereto, without doubt one of us will ; what then shall be our mutual pledge and bond ? ' We answered, ' Be it what you please.' ' Well,' he said, ' let us make a vow, that to whomsoever this fortune falls, he shall share it equally with the rest, and reserve no pre-eminence for himself.' ' Be it so,' we both replied ; and on these terms we mutually pledged our words. Years rolled on, and I went from Khorassan to Transoxiana, and wandered to Ghazni and Cabul ; and when I returned, I was invested with office, and rose to be administrator of affairs during the Sultanate of Sultan Alp Arslan."

The years passed and both his friends came to him in his prosperity and reminded him of youthful vows. He at once gave Hasan a place in the Government. Omar Khayyam did not ask for title or office. " The greatest boon you can confer on me," he said, "is to let me live in a corner under the shadow of your fortune, to spread wide the advantages of Science, and pray for your long life and prosperity." So he was given a pension of 1,200 *mithkals* of gold. " At Naishapur thus lived and died Omar Khayyam, busied," adds the Vizier, " in winning knowledge of every kind, and especially in Astronomy, wherein he attained to a very high pre-eminence. Under the Sultanate of Malik Shah, he came to Merv, and obtained great praise for his proficiency in science, and the Sultan showered favours upon him."

And here amid the roses of Naishapur he wrote his Rubaiyat, at odd times probably, a Ruba'i to-day, another to-morrow, just as the Muse moved him. How many Rubaiyat or verses Omar wrote is not known; the Bodleian MS. from which FitzGerald made his paraphrase contains 158 stanzas, but there are others, containing over 500.

In his translation there is much of FitzGerald, perhaps more than of Omar. Had FitzGerald merely translated we should have had a medley of Eastern colours, the arranging and sorting of which might have been wearisome—even though the colours be perfumed with Persian roses. In passing through the genius of FitzGerald the kaleidoscope has adjusted itself—the reflection of his mind's light has eliminated much obscurity, and we have a priceless gem which certainly owes its lustre and its setting to the Hermit of Boulge.

There is a smooth dignity in the metre—a music that grows on one—a tune of haunting sweetness.

The Rubaiyat is a poem carelessly sceptical, lazily unbelieving, seeking after truth more in playful derision than with any attempt at earnestness. The Astronomer Poet of Naishapur reclined in his garden of roses, enjoying his flask of wine and his loaf of bread with none to gainsay him, viewing things with lackadaisical incredulity. He toys with his scepticism as he does with his bread and his wine and his roses, even thought is burdensome, in fact the whole theme of Omar is of the uselessness of thinking.

FitzGerald not only guides us—he is an artist who paints as he shows, and it is he, rather than Omar, who causes us to dance to the rhythm of the music.

Omar had much in common with FitzGerald; both loved to linger over the sweet memories of the past, both are full of the sorrow that cries out in vain to retain everfleeting joys.

With Poe they murmur his dirge of ever-dying hopes :

> " . . . I hold within my hand
> Grains of the Golden sand
> How few! Yet how they creep
> Through my fingers to the deep,
> While I weep—while I weep!
> O God! can I not grasp
> Them with a tighter clasp ?
> O God ! can I not save
> *One* from the pitiless grave ? "

But with " Omar," if not with FitzGerald, the futility of grasping the sand is recognised. His philosophic dreaming had brought him to recognise that this knot of fate could never be untied, therefore why worry about it ? We have wine, life, to-day,—why think of to-morrow or a future Paradise ? He was very well content to repose voluptuously in his garden of roses with his glass of wine in his hand, delectable dainties by his side and a sweet singer, as beautiful as his other surroundings, to bear him company, and this, though ironically called a wilderness, is Paradise enow!

Because "Omar" cannot find God he does not deny His existence, and though conscious that he will never reach his goal, he goes on searching for it. Though sceptical about the accepted ideas of God, his very search proves his faith. We were not made to be destroyed, as one of the pots in the Potter's shop is made to say:

" . . . Why, ne'er a peevish Boy
Would break the Bowl from which he drank in Joy;
  Shall He that *made* the Vessel in pure Love
And Fancy, in an after Rage destroy!"

Of the earnestness of his seeking and likewise its uselessness, we are assured:

" Myself when young did eagerly frequent
Doctor and Saint, and heard great Argument
  About it and about: but evermore
Came out by the same Door as in I went."

And to that searching there can be no end. The same mystery that puzzled "Omar" eight hundred years ago is a mystery still, and will be for all time.

In the "Omar" Edward FitzGerald found just the outlet that he required for his genius. Here was a sweet melody out of the past, largely in keeping with his own ideas, dealing with love, wine, beauty, the past, and the mysterious future;

epigrammatic, *multum-in-parvo*, stanzas in a rich Oriental setting.

FitzGerald took the poem and interpreted it —with much original thought—into stately, slow-moving English of majestic thought and depth, almost every line an epigram. It comes from his delicate mind a poem, refined, shorn of its sensuousness, and withal sparkling with a new genius; scene after scene passes, like a "Magic Shadow-show," before the reader's eyes, each and every scene set in pure gold.

I have already mentioned how FitzGerald was introduced to Persian by Professor Cowell, and how in the little cottage at Bramford, he, together with Mr. and Mrs. Cowell, loved to pore over the manuscripts. Some time after this, Cowell discovered the "Omar" in the Ouseley collection in the Bodleian Library at Oxford, a priceless manuscript written with purple-black ink, powdered with gold, on yellow paper.

Before Cowell left for India he made a transcript and gave it to FitzGerald, and almost immediately he started in his desultory manner to adapt it. He took it with him on some of his excursions into the country; he writes to Cowell that when on a visit to Bedfordshire, he put all books away except "Omar Khayyam," which he pored over in a buttercup-covered meadow.

Professor Cowell helped him with some of the technical difficulties of the language, and it is evident that FitzGerald experienced much difficulty in getting the true meaning of some of the passages. He writes to Mrs. Cowell asking her to consult her husband on certain points; the line, "*He* knows about it all—He knows—He knows," presented difficulties and he could not get his translated line to scan, so he asks Cowell through his wife to annotate it on the proof sheet.

FitzGerald made many alterations in the editions which followed the first, not thereby it is generally acknowledged improving it, indeed it would seem to be superfluous to paint so fair a lily or gild so perfect a rose, of which Tennyson said:—

> " . . . Your golden Eastern lay,
>   Than which I know no version done
> In English more divinely well;
>   A planet equal to the sun
> Which cast it, that large infidel,
> Your Omar."

And the verdict of Mr. Swinburne is equally laudatory: "As to the greatness of the *Rubaiyat*, I know none to be compared with it for power, pathos, and beauty of thought and work, except possibly Ecclesiastes."

The Rubaiyat has much of the spirit of Ecclesiastes in it, indeed some stanzas might be paraphrases thereof. But Ecclesiastes is a wail of pessimism. Omar's verses are different in this one respect, they are, if not exactly hopeful, full of an inconsequential optimism. The writer of

Ecclesiastes laments that all is vanity. Omar whilst admitting this, laughs, because although unable to solve a riddle which is unsolvable, he delights in those things that his comfortable environment offers.

ECCLESIASTES.	OMAR.
One generation passeth away, And another cometh, But the earth abideth for ever.	Iram indeed is gone with all its Rose And Jamshyd's Sev'n-ring'd Cup where no one knows; But still the Vine her ancient Ruby yields, And still a Garden by the Water blows.
The wise man's eyes are in his head, But the fool walketh in darkness; And I myself perceived also That one event happened to them all.	Why, all the Saints and Sages who discuss'd Of the Two Worlds, so learnedly, are thrust Like foolish Prophets forth; their Words to Scorn Are scattered, and their Mouths are stopt with Dust.
All go unto one place All are of the dust And all turn to dust again.	Ah, make the most of what we yet may spend, Before we too into the Dust descend; Dust into Dust, and under Dust to lie, Sans Wine, sans Song, sans Singer and sans End.
"There is nothing better for a man, than that he should eat and drink, and that he should make his soul enjoy good in his labour." "Go thy way, eat thy bread with joy and drink thy wine with a merry heart."	"Here with a Loaf of Bread beneath the Bough, A Flask of Wine, a book of Verse —and Thou Beside me singing in the Wilderness— And Wilderness is Paradise enow."
	"'How sweet is mortal Sovranty! think some: Others—'How blest the Paradise to come!' Ah, take the Cash in hand and waive the Rest, Oh, the brave Music of a *distant* drum.'

ECCLESIASTES.	OMAR.
"He hath made everything beautiful in his time: also he hath set the world in their heart, so that no man can find out the work that God maketh from the beginning to the end."	"Up from Earth's centre through the Seventh Gate I rose, and on the Throne of Saturn sate, And many Knots unravel'd by the Road; But not the Knot of Human Death and Fate."

The writer of Ecclesiastes, probably Koheleth, teaches that the really wise and only course is to use what we have; to avoid fruitless striving after those things beyond our reach, and to accept the limitations which the very name of man suggests. The whole of man's life is saddened by its brevity. The wisest plan therefore is to labour that we may realise the pleasures of enjoyment, yet even this is vanity.

Omar says much the same sort of thing, he teaches that the one thing certain, is the brevity of life—that life flies, but as we cannot alter it, to enjoy life ere it departs, and not groan over it.

The writer of Ecclesiastes had exceptional advantages for acquiring wisdom, and he made the most of his opportunities, but he could not solve the problem, therefore, what hope can there be for others to do so. The writer of Ecclesiastes and Omar have both found that culture, wisdom and pleasure are good. Yet there is still something wanting to explain the mystery of existence—the enigma of life.

In 1865, FitzGerald published the first edition of *Agamemnon*, a translation or adaptation from the Greek. In this, as in other of his adaptations, FitzGerald has been accused of taking liberties with the original, but the accusation is unjust, as he himself points out it was not his intention, even if he were able, to give a literal translation.

In his preface to *Agamemnon*, he says:

"This grand play, which, to the scholar and the poet, lives, breathes and moves in the dead language, has hitherto seemed to me to drag and stifle under conscientious translation into the living; that is to say, to have lost that which I think the drama can least afford to lose all the world over. And so it was that, hopeless of succeeding where as good versifiers, and better scholars, seemed to me to have failed, I came first to break the bounds of Greek Tragedy; then to swerve from the Master's footsteps; and so, one licence drawing on another to make all of a piece, arrived at the present anomalous conclusion. If it has succeeded in shaping itself into a distinct, consistent and animated whole, through which the reader can follow without halting, and not without accelerating interest from beginning to end, he will perhaps excuse my acknowledged transgressions, and will not disdain the Jade which has carried him so far so well till he finds himself mounted on a Thorough-bred whose thunder-clothed neck and long-resounding pace shall better keep up with the original."

For those who prefer the literal translations there is but one thing to do—get them—or if afraid to trust to the translations of others, there is one other course which does not need naming.

As in so much of FitzGerald's work, *Agamemnon* is fine in certain passages rather than a whole.

In 1868-70, FitzGerald contributed to the *East Anglian Daily Times* a series of contributions signed E. F. G., which largely consisted of the interpretation of Sea-phrases, most of them of Suffolk origin. This was the kind of work that FitzGerald loved: the Suffolk dialect was ever one of his pet hobbies.

I have already quoted from this work, but I reproduce here two other interesting examples:

"'*New Moon*'—When first seen, be sure to turn your money over in your pocket, by way of making it grow there; provided always that you see her face to face, not through a glass (window) —for, in that case, the charm works the wrong way. 'I see the little dear this evening, and give my money a twister; there wasn't much, but I roused her about.' Here '*her*' means the Money, not the Moon. Everyone knows of what gender all that is amiable becomes in the sailor's eyes: his ship, of course the 'Old Dear'—the 'Old Girl'—the 'Old Beauty,' etc. I don't think the sea is so familiarly addrest; *she* is almost too strong-minded, capricious, and terrible a Virago, and—he is wedded to her for better or worse. Yet I have heard the Weather (to whose instigation so much of that Sea's ill-humours are due) spoken of by one coming up the hatchway, 'Let's see how *she* look now.' The Moon is, of course, a Woman too; and as with the German, and, I believe, the ancient Oriental people, 'the blessed Sun himself a fair hot wench in flame colour'd taffeta,' and so *she* rises, *she* sets, and *she* crosses the Line. So the Time-piece that measures the hours of day and night. A Friend's Watch going wrong of late, I advised Regulating; but was gravely answer'd that '*She* was a foreigner, and he did not like meddling with *her*.' The same poor ignorant was looking with me one evening at your fine old Church (Lowestoft), which sadly wanted regulating too: lying all along indeed like a huge stranded ship, with one side battered open to the ribs, through which 'the sea-wind sang shrill, chill'; and he 'did not like seeing *her* so distress'd'; remembering boyish days, and her good old Vicar (of course I mean the *former* one: pious, charitable, venerable Francis Cunningham), and looking to lie under her walls, among his own people—'if not,' as he said, '*somewhere else*.' Some months after, seeing the Church with her southern side restored to the sun, the same speaker cried, 'Well done, Old Girl! Up, and crow again!'"

"'*Brustle*'—A compound of *Bustle* and *Rustle*, I suppose. 'Why, the old girl *brustle* along like a Hedge-sparrow!'—said of a round-bowed vessel spuffing through the water. I am told that, comparing little with great, the figure is not out of the way. Otherwise, what should these ignorant seamen know of Hedge-sparrows? Some of them do, however; fond of birds, as of other pets—children, cats, small dogs—anything in short, considerably under the size of—a bullock—and accustomed to bird's-nesting over your cliff and about your lanes from childhood. A little while ago a party of Beechmen must needs have a day's frolic at the old sport; marching bodily into a neighbouring farmer's domain, ransacking the hedges, climbing the trees, coming down pretty figures, I was told (in plainer language), with guernsey and breeches torn fore and aft; the farmer after them in a tearing rage, calling for his gun—'They were Pirates—They were the Press-gang!' and the boys in blue going on with their game laughing. When they had got their fill of it, they adjourned to Oulton Boar for 'Half-a-pint'; by-and-bye in came the raging farmer for a like purpose: at first growling aloof; then warming towards the good fellows, till he joined their company, and insisted on paying their shot."

I quote these because they shew another side of the character of the translator of "Omar Khayyam"—a kindly, simple side, which did so much to endear him to the hearts of Suffolk folk.

But FitzGerald's fame, apart from "Omar," undoubtedly rests upon his Letters. In them the tender, retrospective, wistful dreamer reveals his true self. They are human documents, phrenological charts, by means of which we talk without embarrassment to him, and in the talking we come to know and love the man. Carlyle thought so and writes to him :

"Thanks for your friendly human letter, which gave us much entertainment in the reading (at breakfast time the other day) and is still pleasant to think of. One gets so many *in*human letters—ovine, bovine, porcine, etc., etc. I wish you would write a little oftener. When the beneficent Daimon suggests, fail not to lend ear to him."

His letters are full of picturesque descriptions, quiet humour, gentle, almost inapparent, criticisms, stately diction and at times pathos. They are deliberate letters, never hasty, never careless : he just talks to us in his charming, indolent way.

His letters abound in the most delightful criticisms of art, music and literature, and it is noteworthy that what he said to-day the world said to-morrow.

With an insight that was intuition he at once recognises the imperfections of a poem, a book or a picture, and in the simplest possible manner he just says what he thinks about them, and only rarely is the steel behind the velvet felt. His criticism is kindly, at times humorous, always casual, and intended more for the entertainment of his correspondents than for a serious attempt at making public the imperfections of the man, poem, book or picture criticised.

* * * *

A man is best judged by the opinions of his intimates, and the friends of FitzGerald, without a single exception, speak of him with deep love, almost reverence. His charities were numerous and generous, but known only to the recipients. He was tender-hearted and ingenuous, the kindest of hosts, providing his friends with the very best, whilst he himself would pace up and down the room munching an apple and taking long draughts of milk. "He was no Sybarite. There was a vein of strong scorn of self-indulgence in him, which was very different. He was, of course, very much of a recluse, with a vein of misanthropy towards men in the abstract, joined to a tender-hearted sympathy for the actual men and women around him. He was the very reverse of Carlyle's description of the sentimental philanthropist, who loves man in the abstract, but is intolerant of 'Jack and Tom, who have wills of their own.'"

Edward FitzGerald, as I have pointed out, had much in common with Omar of Naishapur; many traits found in Koheleth, the probable writer of Ecclesiastes, and in Lucretius, were also shared by FitzGerald, but the sensuous element, of which Omar Khayyam, Koheleth and Lucretius boasted, was not found in FitzGerald, the disciple of the simple life. The only passion to which he pandered, was a worship of the beautiful—flowers, sunsets, rivers and woods; beauty in art and literature; to him a primrose was a text for a sermon, a rose a benediction and a good book a beatitude.

*   *   *   *

So back to Boulge again, the end of it so far as the man himself is concerned, back to the roses, back to the quiet and peace of his sleeping-place: stand in the shadow of the Church tower just now as evening falls and the shadow reaches the large cross on his grave. It is one of his sunsets, his spirit stirs in the roses and presently the nightingales will begin to sing in the flowering chestnuts of Boulge.

EDWARD FITZGERALD'S LETTERS.

By Alfred Ainger.

MUCH has been said of late years respecting the publication of letters—intimate and friendly—following soon after the death of their writer. And, indeed, the action of certain editors and literary executors within recent experience has done much to justify severe criticism, and, as Lord Brougham said of a well-known legal biographer of his day, to "add a new terror to death." But as certainly the above-named addition to the "Library of Familiar Correspondence" will not deepen the outcry against such literature. In "The Letters of Edward FitzGerald," the cherished friend of Tennyson, Spedding, Thackeray, and William Bodham Donne, as given to the world under the editorial care of Mr. Aldis Wright, a single sentence here and there might well have been omitted; but for the rest it is no more than truth to say that the world is made richer by a charming book, and that not one of FitzGerald's friends is the poorer for a disparaging or unkind word to be therein found. Of disparaging words the letters, indeed, contain not a few. FitzGerald was full of words: he had his genial days and his ungenial: he did not appreciate the same book equally on different occasions. Not only did he often illustrate the converse of Benedick's remark that a man may "love the meat in his youth that he cannot endure in his age," but his judgments often varied from month to month. It is, in fact, one of the charms of a biography told in letters that the man is seen " in the making." FitzGerald is known to us, with scarce the aid of a biographer at all, more perfectly and more delightfully than any other the most cunning hand could have drawn him.

These letters will make Edward FitzGerald a dear and cherished personality to thousands who will never care for his verse or prose—to whom even the consummate versification of Omar Khayyam will not atone for its defiant epicureanism, and who will never become acclimatised to Calderon, or reconciled to adaptations of Aeschylus. No letters of such variety of charm have been given to the world since Charles Lamb's. The comparison is inevitable for more than one reason. Both men had a rare critical faculty, exercised without fear or favour, and independently of all cliques and coteries. Each had developed a style of his own, based on those older authors he had loved and assimilated. Each had the keenest sense of humour and the tenderest of loyal hearts for his friends. Among the chief differences between the two, FitzGerald's love of the country, with its charms of bird-haunted lawns and flower beds is everywhere apparent. In this respect it is Cowper, and perhaps White of Selborne, who will oftenest recur to the reader. But there is much in the letters absolutely individual, and outside of all possible comparison with others. A singularly attractive personality has been added to the catalogue of English writers.

His fate has been a curious one. Save to a small group of poets, scholars, and artists, his name was during his lifetime unknown. His only production that attained any celebrity—the Quatrains of Omar Khayyam—was published anonymously. The history of its success is another commentary on Mr. Puff's most just observation that the number of those who take the trouble of judging for themselves is exceedingly small. The little pamphlet, printed by Mr. Quaritch, bearing no name, and with no godfather to vouch for it, soon fell into the sixpenny box; and though many must have seen it, few dared to think it good and to predict its fame, until it came accidentally into the hands of one or two poets and scholars with a real feeling for what is genuine. Once and once only, did FitzGerald attach his name to a volume —the six plays of Calderon. But the result was not such as to encourage a repetition of the practice. The plays were cut and carved, and the jests of the comic servants were increased by some of FitzGerald's own, and these liberties are just what the rigid critic is most intolerant of. The wrong done to the Spanish classic was remembered; and the poetic beauty and vivacity of the translator passed without praise. FitzGerald was fastidious and sensitive. He does not seem to have cared for fame, except in the form of approval from those he loved. His versatility of taste and faculty would in any case have kept him from being soured by the absence of public appreciation. In him the critic savoured not in the least of the author who had failed. He was fastidious in his estimate of others, as he was in judging himself. It is difficult indeed to understand how with his fine appreciation of Lord Tennyson's earlier poems he should have failed to recognise what was of sterling truth and beauty in "In Memoriam" and the Arthurian Idylls. But it is clear that his judgment in all such cases was absolutely free from unworthy motive, even when, as sometimes, it depended on the mood of the hour.

"I had no truer friend," wrote the late Poet Laureate to the late Sir Frederick Pollock, on hearing of FitzGerald's death, "he was one of the kindliest of men." It is plain that the inability of FitzGerald to approve equally all of Lord Tennyson's verse had not estranged the person most nearly affected. And, indeed, in the criticism of a man who really judges for himself, without fear or favour, there is no real sting. And when FitzGerald praised the discernment of his praise outweighed all censure. For there was always something of the prophet in FitzGerald's, as in all fine criticism. As early as the eve of the publication of Tennyson's second little volume in 1833, he foretells the chastening and strengthening of his friend's powers :—

"Tennyson has been in town for some time: he has been making fresh poems, which are finer, they say, than any he has done. But I believe he is chiefly meditating on the purging and subliming of what he has already done; and repents that he has published at all yet. It is fine to see how in each succeeding poem the smaller ornaments and fancies drop away, and leave the grand ideas single."

A better thing could hardly have been better said in this last sentence, which notes how the verbal ingenuities of those earliest lyrics were destined to give place to profounder harmonies in the future. The same prophetic insight into the development of Tennyson's genius is shown in a letter of three years later to Mr. (afterwards Archdeacon) Allen, who had apparently been lamenting that Tennyson's poetry showed less "of conscience and of aim" than Wordsworth's :—

"What you say of Tennyson and Wordsworth is not, I think, wholly just. I don't think that a man can turn himself so directly to the service of morality, unless naturally inclined. I think Wordsworth's is a natural bias that way. Besides, we must have labourers of different kinds in the vineyard of morality, which I certainly look up to as the chief object of our cultivation. Wordsworth is first in the craft; but Tennyson does no little by raising and filling the brain with noble images and thoughts, which, if they do not direct us to our duty, purify and cleanse us from mean and vicious objects, and so prepare and fit us for the reception of the higher philosophy. A man might forsake a drunken party to read Byron's 'Corsair,' and Byron's 'Corsair' for Shelley's 'Alastor,' and the 'Alastor' for the 'Dream of Fair Women' or the 'Palace of Art': and then I won't say he would forsake these two last for anything of Wordsworth's, but his mind would be sufficiently refined and spiritualised to admit Wordsworth, and profit by him, and he might keep all the former imaginations as so many pictures, or pieces of music, in his mind. But I think that you will see Tennyson acquire all that at present you miss: when he has *felt* life he will not die fruitless of instruction to man as he is. But I dislike this kind of criticism, especially in a letter. I don't know any one who has thought out anything so little as I have. I don't see to any end, and should keep silent till I have got a little more, and that little better arranged."

Very significant is this passage of FitzGerald's real genius for criticism, and of his genuine modesty with it. He was a young man of six-and-twenty when he wrote these words. Tennyson was of nearly the same age, and the volumes of 1842 were as yet seven years distant. When they appeared, with the " Two Voices," the " Morte d'Arthur," and the " Vision of Sin," FitzGerald's prediction was amply fulfilled. It is indeed strange that in uttering this prediction the writer should have, as it were, apologised for not " seeing to any end."

Another instance of this critical insight going straight to the mark is afforded in FitzGerald's remarks upon " Selections" from great prose writers as failing to convey any true impression of their real greatness. Basil Montague had edited a collection of Passages from the old English Divines, and FitzGerald writes to John Allen :—

" A single selection from Jeremy Taylor is fine ; but it requires a skilful hand to put many detached bits from him together; for a common editor only picks out the flowery, metaphorical morsels, and so rather cloys, and gives quite a wrong estimate of the author to those who had no previous acquaintance with him. For, rich as Taylor's illustrations, and grotesque as his images are, no one keeps a grander proportion ; he never huddles illustration upon the matter so as to overlay it, nor crowds images too thick together, which these selections might make anyone unacquainted with him to suppose. This is always the fault of selections; but

Taylor is particularly liable to injury on this score."

A criticism, both in matter and in manner, recalling Charles Lamb. The Letters are rich in such from end to end, and their value, as in Lamb's case, is really due to the writer's isolation from critical cliques, and from all fashions and temporary conventions in criticism. How well he understood the ways and weaknesses of the professional critic is shown in many a pungent observation. When Tennyson's two volumes of 1842 appeared, he pointed out immediately that one little vanity such as "The Skipping Rope" would be the fly in the apothecary's ointment to many a "reviewer and dull reader," and retard the right appreciation of the book for a dozen years—just as "The Idiot Boy" had hindered Wordsworth's recognition for a like term. But "some of the poems" (he adds, in a somewhat earlier letter, with a delicate sarcasm) "will outlive the reviewers." A yet more trenchant sarcasm, by the way, occurs in the same letter. "Milnes, I hear, talks of publishing a *popular* edition of his poems. He means a cheap one."

Among other wrong impressions that might too easily be formed from FitzGerald's frequent apologetic references to his leisurely life and the absence of any aims usually called practical, would be this, that his leisure meant idleness, and that the consciousness of talents unemployed was the key to the melancholy of his later years. The very excellence of his verse and prose alike might confirm the impression. Both are so lucid and so apparently effortless as easily to mislead those who have never learned the precious truth as to the relations of hard writing and easy reading. At thirty years of age, in the prime of his powers, ne describes, with a felicity of phrase that Cowper never surpassed, how scholarship and the happy "garden state" satisfied all his needs, at least when the weather was fine:—

"Here is a glorious sunshiny day: all the morning I read about Nero in Tacitus, lying at full length on a bench in the garden: a nightingale singing, and some red anemones eyeing the sun manfully not far off. A funny mixture all this: Nero and the delicacy of spring: all very human, however. Then at half-past one lunch on Cambridge cream cheese: then a ride over hill and dale: then spudding up some weeds from the grass: and then coming in I sit down to write to you, my sister, winding red worsted from the back of a chair, and the most delightful little girl in the world chattering incessantly. So runs the world away. You think I live in Epicurean ease; but this happens to be a jolly day: one isn't always well, or tolerably good, the weather is not always clear, nor nightingales singing, nor Tacitus full of pleasant atrocity. But such as life is, I believe I have got hold of a good end of it."

Where had FitzGerald acquired the masterly ease of this description? Certainly not from the Epicureanism of it. The translator of Omar Khayyam was "makin' himsel'" all this time, like Sir Walter Scott. Both the Tacitus and the nightingales were entering into his blood. If he idled it was not to read the latest three-volume novel. It was by no indolence that a style was being formed that shaped itself, when time was ripe, in stanzas such as these:—

> I sometimes think that never blows so red
> The Rose, as where some buried Cæsar bled;
> That every Hyacinth the garden wears
> Dropt in his Lap from some once lovely Head.
>
> And this delightful Herb, whose tender green
> Fledges the River's Lip on which we lean—
> Ah! lean upon it lightly! for who knows
> From what once lovely lip it springs unseen;
>
> Ah my Belovèd, fill the Cup that clears
> TO-DAY of past Regrets and future Fears—
> To-morrow? Why, to-morrow I may be
> Myself with yesterday's Seven Thousand Years.

Would the discipline of a profession or other compulsory occupation have enabled FitzGerald to make more of his undoubted gifts, and to concentrate them on some more enduring work? It would be dangerous to dogmatise on this head. The country, even in the homelier aspects it wears in Bedfordshire and Suffolk, encouraged and fostered the individuality of which FitzGerald was conscious. Whenever he tried a change to London, though it gave him happy meetings with Thackeray and Spedding and William Bodham Donne, he found his better powers in danger there. "One finds few in London *serious* men," he writes to Frederick Tennyson in 1844. "I mean *serious* even in fun: with a true purpose and character whatsoever it may be. London melts away all individuality into a common lump of cleverness. I am amazed at the humour and worth and noble feeling in the country, however much railroads have mixed us up with metropolitan civilisation. I can still find the heart of England beating healthily down here, though no one will believe it."

The "here" is Boulge, near Woodbridge. In mentioning the place to another correspondent he observes that the very sound suggests a good stiff clay. Yet to the poet's eye nothing is commonplace, and after just lamenting the monotony of London cleverness he goes on, with an evident sense of relief, to expatiate on the infinite variety of nature, that never tires:—
"I read of mornings: the same old books over and over again, having no command of new ones: walk with my great black dog of an afternoon, and at evening sit with open windows, up which China roses climb, with my pipe, while the blackbirds and thrushes begin to rustle bedwards in the garden, and the nightingale to have the neighbourhood to herself. We have had such a spring (bating the last ten days) as would

have satisfied even *you* with warmth. And such verdure! white clouds moving over the new-fledged tops of oak trees, and acres of grass striving with buttercups. How old to tell of, how new to see!" "Daddy Wordsworth," as FitzGerald and his friends loved to nickname the poet, could hardly have surpassed this, and the Letters are full of such delicate and tender studies of life in the country. FitzGerald has in prose done for the scenery of the Deben what Cowper did in verse for that of the Ouse, and with a large portion of Cowper's own spirit.

A charm, which I venture to predict will outlast the changes of fashion, pervades these Letters. It is an instructive lesson in the conditions of permanent and ephemeral popularity to contrast the attractiveness of this record of a quiet student's life with that of the hundred and one volumes of reminiscences and autobiographies of the last few years, which have had their day and already ceased to be. At the root of all permanence for such books is the quality of tenderness, the revelation of a loving and faithful human soul. It is Fitz-Gerald's unselfishness and pitifulness for the commonest human forms about him—his feeling for all that was tender and noble in others that draws the reader more and more closely to the writer of these letters, till, when he arrives at the close, he finds that he has come to know and to feel that he has lost a friend. There are few things in biography or in fiction more touching than the glimpse (it is little more) here given of the old captain of the herring boat with whom FitzGerald went into partnership out of a simple desire to help financially a neighbour, whose character he had come to love and honour.

"I have come here," he writes to his friend Cowell from Lowestoft, "to wind up accounts for our herring lugger: much against us, as the season has been a bad one. My dear captain, who looks in his cottage like King Alfred in the story, was rather saddened by all this, as he had prophesied better things. I tell him that if he is but what I think him—and, surely, my sixty years of considering men will not so undeceive me at last!—I would rather lose money with him than gain it with others. Indeed, I never proposed gain, as you may imagine, but only to have some interest with this dear fellow."

And a year later he again writes to Cowell from Woodbridge:—" My lugger captain has just left me to go on his mackerel voyage to the Western coast; and I don't know when I shall see him again. Just after he went a muffled bell from the church here began to toll for somebody's death; it sounded like a bell under the sea. He sat listening to the hymn played by the church chimes last evening, and said he could hear it all as if in Lowestoft Church when he was a boy, 'Jesus, our Deliverer.' You can't think what a grand, tender soul this is, lodged in a suitable carcase."

Exquisite and original as these Letters are, I have reason to think that they are far from widely known even to that limited public which is best fitted to enjoy them. So little adventurous are people in finding out and cherishing the best in literature, so eager to sustain the chorus of praise for that which is less worthy. It is cheering to note, on the other hand, how quick the born letter writer is to recognise the kindred gift in others. The late Mr. T. E. Brown, of Clifton College, the poet of the "Foc'sle Yarns," and of much else of rarer poetical beauty, in his Letters writes with no exaggeration of FitzGerald when he says, "There is an ἦθος in FitzGerald's letters which is so exquisitely idyllic as to be almost heavenly. He takes you with him, exactly *accommodating* his pace to yours, walks through meadows so tranquil and yet abounding in the most delicate surprises. . . . What delicious blending! What a perfect interweft of thought and diction! What a *sweet* companion!"

Mr. Aldis Wright, FitzGerald's literary executor, has given us a little "Golden Treasury" volume (Macmillan) of shorter pieces of FitzGerald, some of which had not been yet reprinted, including the Memoir of Bernard Barton, the Preface to the Selections from

Crabbe and others. Among them two lyrics of great beauty from the latter of which (on the Death of a Miss Anne Allen) I may be allowed to quote the two last stanzas, which will, I am sure, send my readers to the little volume itself :—

> Her pleasant smile spread sunshine upon all;
> We heard her sweet, clear laughter in the hall;
>   Vanity of vanities, the Preacher saith.
> We heard her sometimes after evening prayer,
> As she went singing softly up the stair—
>   No voice can charm thee, Death.
>
> Where is the pleasant smile, the laughter kind
> That made sweet music of the winter wind?
>   Vanity of vanities, the Preacher saith.
> Idly they gaze upon her empty place.
> Her kiss hath faded from her father's face—
>   She is with thee, O Death.

INDEX.

Agamemnon, 151
Aldeburgh, 8, 56, 84
Allen (Anne), 29, 30
Allen (John), 26

Barton (Bernard), 1, 2, 3, 35, 43, 72
Beccles, 25
Bibliography, 111, 112
Bird Parliament, 127
Bloomfield (Robert), 1, 2, 10, 11
Bodleian Library, 147
Boulge Cottage, 7
Boulge Hall, 7, 32
Boy Readers, 70, 71, 80, 90, 91, 93
Bramford, 9, 40
Bredfield House, 6, 20, 21
Browne (W. K.), 39, 62
Bull Hotel, Woodbridge, 18
Bunyan Meeting House, Bedford, 19
Bury St. Edmunds, 10, 11, 12

Carlyle, 55, 56, 57, 83
Castle Irwell, 20
Cowell (E. B.), 2, 9, 39, 40, 57, 58, 147
Crabbe (Caroline), 8, 9, 33, 43, 85
Crabbe (George, *poet*), 1, 2, 8, 25, 29
Crabbe (George, *son of poet*), 32, 62

Debach, 41
Dickens (C.), 1
Dunwich, 71

Ecclesiastes, 148, 149
Euphranor, 121

Farlingay Hall, 7
FitzGerald (Edward)
 birth, 15
 brothers and sisters, 16
 opinion of his brother, 19
 goes to Paris, 21
 attends private school at Woodbridge, 22
 at school at Bury, 22
 entered at Trinity College, Cambridge, 22
 at College, 23, 24
 visits his sister, 25
 visits Paris with Thackeray, 25
 goes to Naseby, 26
 Meadows in Spring, 26
 back to Bredfield, 27
 visits Lowestoft, 27
 To a Lady Singing, 29
 stays at Bedford, 31
 lake district, 31
 Boulge Hall, 31
 visits Geldestone Hall, 33
 moves to Boulge Cottage, 34
 friendship with Carlyle, 36
 visits Ireland, 37
 anecdote, 41
 contributes to *Ipswich Journal*, 43, 44, 45, 46, 47, 48, 49
 Euphranor, 51
 visits Prees, 52
 Polonius, 53
 Calderon's Plays, 53
 moves to Farlingay Hall, 54
 Oxford, 55
 Carlyle's visit, 56
 his marriage, 58
 Persian studies, 61
 returns to Woodbridge, 62
 moves to Market Place, Woodbridge, 63
 anecdote, 64
 Wiltshire, 65
 buys Little Grange 65
 the *Scandal*, 65
 friendship with "Posh," 66, 67
 contributes to *East Anglian Daily Times*, 67, 152, 153, 154
 moves to Little Grange, 74
 visits Scotland, 77

INDEX.

his favourite books, 80
Lowestoft, 80
London, 81
sees *Hamlet*, 81
Crabbe's *Tales of the Hall*, 82
visits Mrs. Kemble, 83
Merton Rectory, 83
visits the Cowells, 84
bequests, 84
death, 86
funeral, 86
characteristics, 88
anecdote, 88, 89, 91
his generosity, 94
anecdote, 95
his humour, 95, 96
politics, 97
personal appearance, 98
anecdote, 99
favourite authors, 102
religious views, 103
friendships, 104, 105, 106, 107
FitzGerald (John), 12, 17, 18, 19, 68, 82
FitzGerald (John Purcell), 15
his extravagance, 21
death, 53
FitzGerald (Mrs. Edward), 59, 60
FitzGerald (Mary Frances), 16, 20, 24, 55

Gorleston, 61
Groome (Archdeacon), 13, 19, 79

Honington, 10
Howe (John and Mary), 76

Ipswich, 1, 2, 78
Ipswich Journal, 79

Jenny (Squire), 51, 52

Keene (Charles), 6, 79, 109
Kemble (Fanny), 52, 75, 76
Koheleth, 150

Lamb (Charles), 4, 11, 27
Letters, 155, 159 *et seq.*
Little Grange, 67, 68
Loder (John), 33, 108
Lynn (Mary), 84

Matthews (Rev. T. R.), 19, 37, 38
Merton Rectory, 11

Naseby, 20

Omar Khayyam, Life of, 141, 142, 143
Omar Khayyam, 146, 147, 148
Ouida, 11

Playford, 13
Poe, 145
Poetry, *To my daughter, Bernard Barton*, 45
   In Memoriam of Bernard Barton, FitzGerald, 51
   Tiresias, quoted, 79
   Meadows in Spring, 113
   To a Lady Singing, 116
   The Old Beau, 117
   Bredfield Hall, 118
Polonius, 123
Pollock (F.), 96
Portland Place, 20
"Posh," 66, 69

Reydon Hall, 12
Rubaiyat, 63, 128, *et seq.*
Rubaiyat, Remarks on, 144
Rubaiyat and *Ecclesiastes*, 149, 150

Salaman and Absal, 126
Seaford, 20
Smith (Job), 7, 54
Southey (R.), 13
Strickland (Agnes), 12
Suffolk Sayings, 92
Swinburne, 148

Tennyson (Alfred), 23, 31, 77, 78, 90, 148
Tennyson (Frederick), 23, 35
Thackeray, 23, 65
Two Suffolk Friends, 28

Wade (Thos.), 5
Wherstead Lodge, 22
Wolsey (Cardinal), 1
Woodbridge, 3, 5
Wright (W. Aldis), 25, 69

BIBLIOLIFE

Old Books Deserve a New Life
www.bibliolife.com

Did you know that you can get most of our titles in our trademark **EasyScript**™ print format? **EasyScript**™ provides readers with a larger than average typeface, for a reading experience that's easier on the eyes.

Did you know that we have an ever-growing collection of books in many languages?

Order online:
www.bibliolife.com/store

Or to exclusively browse our **EasyScript**™ collection:
www.bibliogrande.com

At BiblioLife, we aim to make knowledge more accessible by making thousands of titles available to you – quickly and affordably.

Contact us:
BiblioLife
PO Box 21206
Charleston, SC 29413

Lightning Source UK Ltd.
Milton Keynes UK
UKHW021840010719
345378UK00025B/719/P